Keep the Fire Burning
The Folk Mass Revolution

by
Ken Canedo

Foreword by
Father Virgil Funk

Pastoral Press
Portland, Oregon

Keep the Fire Burning: THE FOLK MASS REVOLUTION
Ken Canedo

ISBN 978-1-56929-083-5

© 2009 Pastoral Press
All rights reserved.
An imprint of OCP
5536 NE Hassalo Street
Portland, OR 97213-3638
Phone: 1-800-LITURGY (548-8749)
E-mail: liturgy@ocp.org
web: ocp.org

Publisher: John J. Limb
Director of Editorial Processes: Eric Schumock
Director of Artist Relations and Product Development: Tom Tomaszek
Project Editor: Bari Colombari
Editing Assistance: Nancy Wolf
Book Layout: Stephanie Miller
Art Direction and Cover Design: Judy Urben

Cover photograph montage (clockwise from bottom left): John Fischer; The Paul Quinlan Trio (Rich Regan, Paul Quinlan, Steve Seery); Ray Repp; Sebastian Temple; Peter Scholtes and members of the St. Brendan Choir; Carey Landry; Glenmary Sister Germain Habjan; Jack Miffleton; The Dameans (Dave Baker, Darryl Ducote, Mike Balhoff, Buddy Ceasar, Gary Ault)

Printed in the United States of America

Contents

Acknowledgments 5

Foreword by Father Virgil Funk 7

Introduction by Ken Canedo:
"Come, Gather 'Round, People, Wherever You Roam" 9

Chapter One:
"Pange Lingua Gloriosi" 11

Chapter Two:
"Hang Down Your Head, Tom Dooley" 17

Chapter Three:
"Veni, Creator Spiritus" 23

Chapter Four:
"God Is Love" 31

Chapter Five:
"Keep the Fire Burning" 41

Chapter Six:
Mass for Young Americans 49

Chapter Seven:
"Wake Up, My People" 57

Photo Album:
"Memories" 67

Chapter Eight:
Hymnal for Young Christians 71

Chapter Nine:
"They'll Know We Are Christians" 79

Chapter Ten:
"We Shall Overcome" 93

Chapter Eleven:
"Sing, People of God, Sing" 105

Chapter Twelve:
"Glory Land" 113

Chapter Thirteen:
The Time Has Not Come True 121

Epilogue:
"Is There Any Word?" 135

Acknowledgments

Dedicated to Roger Nachtwey, 1930–2007, a genuine Catholic music pioneer whose dedication to liturgical reform helped pave the way for the Folk Mass.

▪

This book required six years of research and writing but it seems a lifetime in the making. First I thank my mother, Victorina Canedo, for giving me life and for being such an inspiring example of faith. I was a child in the pre-Vatican II Church and sang Gregorian chant in our parish children's choir, so I am deeply indebted to the priests and nuns at Saint Gerard Majella Church in Los Angeles who nurtured my love for liturgy and for music. At all levels of my education the music teachers at school opened up the wonders of music theory for me and I am grateful. During my college years I somehow ended up working for FEL Publications and my life became forever linked with liturgical music. For that I give thanks to Dennis Fitzpatrick, Thomas Cook, and the late Roger Nachtwey, all of whom generously shared stories and ideas from back in the day.

As someone who grew up in the Catholic music industry, the biggest thrill in writing this book was connecting with the composers who inspired me. You will read their contributions. I especially thank the following composers who shared themselves so generously: Ray Repp, Carey Landry, Jack Miffleton, the Dameans (especially Gary Ault, Dave Baker, and Buddy Ceasar), John Fischer, and Mercy Sister Suzanne Toolan. Thanks also to Rich Regan of the Paul Quinlan Trio and Sarah Hershberg, without whom I would not have uncovered the story of Sebastian Temple. I'm grateful also to Bruce Bruno for the wonderful memories he shared of his late father, Ray Bruno. To everyone I interviewed, thank you.

I give thanks to John Limb and Tom Tomaszek of OCP for their encouragement and constant support, to Pamela Gigliotti for her assistance, to Barbara Bridge, my project liaison at OCP, and to Bari Colombari, my editor at Pastoral Press. Special thanks to Father Virgil Funk for his insightful ideas and suggestions and for his Foreword. I also thank Benedictine Father Godfrey Mullen, whose dissertation, *Participation in the Liturgy: The National Liturgical Weeks 1940–1962*, helped guide my research. I am grateful to Bob Hurd, who took a chance on this scrappy piano player back in the 1970s and changed my life. Thanks also to Joe Griffith and Kevin Ward for their moral support over the years. Lastly, I thank my friend Phillip J. Signey who lived this story with me through high school, college, and beyond. Without him, this book would not be possible.

▪

This is a book about music. While those of a certain generation will "hear" the melodies of the songs cited, many others will not have the benefit of this music memory. I invite you to access my website, www.kencanedo.com, to hear music podcasts related to the phenomenon of the Folk Mass.

Foreword

The Folk Mass — what is your reaction when you hear that expression? Does it stir memories of your youth, playing at the late-night liturgy in college? Or maybe the first time you made music with a few strums on a guitar? Perhaps you are old enough to remember the battle between organ and guitar, where you had to choose which Mass to attend because of the music. Do you remember what else was going on in the United States at that time — the civil rights movement, the assassinations of the Kennedys and Martin Luther King, Jr.? And can you remember the mixed emotions expressed by various leaders in the Catholic Church, not only about the Folk Mass, but about English in the liturgy and singing in liturgy? Some were enthusiastic, some were highly resistant, and some were just uncertain about where all this was going to lead!

The reaction then was based on your ear — what you heard as religious music and what you heard as music. If you were a trained musician, the "autobiography of your ear" (i.e., your musical training and your musical orientation) more than likely turned you away from four-chord guitar playing in an instant. But if your ear was trained by the protest movement that surrounded many college campuses, you probably looked for a liturgy that celebrated the social message absorbing you at the time, and you found what came to be called the Folk Mass.

And today, when you open this book and see the title *Keep the Fire Burning: The Folk Mass Revolution,* is it any different? Ken Canedo has written a history of the Folk Mass revolution and he has done all of us — classically trained musicians, formally trained liturgists, parish priests, conservatives, liberals, folk musicians, or whatever label you attach to the "autobiography of your ear" — he has done all of us an immense service by having written an honest, though clearly slanted, history of the Folk Mass in the United States between the years 1960 and 1970, and he has written it from various perspectives. Perhaps the most interesting is from the perspective of the composers: Ray Repp, Carey Landry, Joe Wise, the Dameans, and more. Ken has deliberately combined the history of the music composed for the liturgy with the music composed for religious education and called it the Folk Mass because that is how it was used! Through interviews with many of the composers, he has captured their intentions, which were often quite different from how their music was used. The book includes very personal and lively stories.

The author has set the music in the context of the times and the Church's urgent post-Vatican II demand for vernacular songs. Often forgotten is the lack of definitive liturgical leadership by the Catholic bishops. "Instant" music emerged because no other way was proposed. We now realize that it was not the composers and the parishes reaching out to embrace the "new" that produced the "instant music" revolution. It was that the other options were not supported or did not work. The bishops returning from the euphoria of the Second Vatican Council's renewal legislation frankly overlooked the importance of the repertoire, the musicians who led it, and the composers who created it. There was no experimental testing done with the new liturgy. It is no surprise that the wave of social movements swirling outside the church doors was used as a source for parish worship music.

Ken Canedo worked for FEL Publications in the early 1970s, and he has written his history with a large dose of the story of that one publisher — its rise and fall — and that's okay. While the Folk Mass was not the only music that was being sung during this period, and while many parishes never allowed the Folk Mass or guitars, many did, and the music published and promoted by FEL was at the center of that movement. Consequently, the centrality of FEL in this story is appropriate, even though, as Ken mentions, several other major Catholic publishers also built their repertoire during that period.

But Ken has also has written a book that provides the opportunity for serious reflection on the story of the Folk Mass. In 1967, the broad liturgical directives issued by ecclesial leadership attempted to provide guidance by including some popular music and excluding others, based mainly on textual consideration. The directives did speak of musical issues, but few listened. Why? Because the Church leadership was looking for "instant" music that encouraged the assembly to sing along, mistakenly identifying singing with active participation. This book provides an opportunity to reflect on the current questions facing every pastoral musician in every parish liturgy: What is the entertainment value of the music and when does it dominate the liturgical function of the celebrations? The Carnegie Hall performance of Folk Mass music sponsored by C.J. McNaspy gives some clues. Ken Canedo appropriately asks the reader to reflect on the key questions: Was it folk music and was it liturgical? And he gives his answers in Chapter 11.

In 1976, when the National Association of Pastoral Musicians (NPM) was founded, some identified it exclusively with the folk movement. As NPM's founder, I never did. Pastoral music was much larger. But I am happy to state that the folk movement was indeed an important precursor to NPM and this book will clearly show you why. The Folk Mass was a formative era of teaching the assembly to sing. The mistakes are informative, too: singing at Mass, singing "songs," searching for "hit tunes," and an abundance of publisher-driven repertoire. *Keep the Fire Burning* provides the opportunity to reflect on both the good and the bad of the era.

If you are a classically trained musician, you should read this book. The "autobiography of your ear" will make it a challenging read, but it is worth the effort. If you are a young musician playing in an eclectic ensemble in your parish, you should read this book. It will give some sense of the history and the people whose efforts made it possible for you to play the music you do today. If you are a non-musician pastor (or bishop), you should read this book. It will provide some perspective that may keep us from making the same mistakes that were made during the 1960s. If you are over 60, you should read this book — for the pure delight of reliving much of your own liturgical music history. And you can laugh, as Ken does, on the bus ride home.

Reverend Virgil C Funk,
President Emeritus
National Association of Pastoral Musicians
Holy Thursday, April 9, 2009

Introduction
"Come, Gather 'Round, People, Wherever You Roam"

> Let the word go forth from this time and place, to friend and foe alike, that the torch has been passed to a new generation of Americans.... The energy, the faith, the devotion which we bring to this endeavor will light our country and all those who serve it — and the glow from that fire can truly light the world.
>
> —Inaugural Address of President John. F. Kennedy
> January 20, 1961

> "Keep the fire burning; kindle it with care…"
>
> —"Here We Are," Ray Repp 1966

Countless volumes have been written about the social and historical phenomenon known as the 1960s. Known variously as the Soaring Sixties, the Swinging Sixties, the Turbulent Decade, or That Damn Decade, mere mention of the 1960s conjures vivid images: civil rights marches in Selma and Washington; children in Vietnam running fearfully from the ravages of war; throngs of music-loving hippies at Woodstock; astronauts romping on the moon; and, perhaps most poignantly, a toddler's heart-tugging salute for his fallen presidential father.

The Sixties certainly saw upheaval in almost every field, from politics and race relations to education, science, entertainment, art, and morality. Religion was not immune to this unrest, and the Catholic Church was particularly affected, with priests and nuns abandoning their vows in unprecedented numbers. Catholics wondered what would become of the Church as members of their own clergy were linked with the experimentation and "new morality" of the day.

By the end of the decade, Americans were numbed by the television images beamed into their living rooms every night: political assassinations, urban riots, campus demonstrations, and the endless escalation of bloodshed in Vietnam. It was hard to believe that the Sixties began with bright promise.

Both President John Kennedy (1917–1963) and Pope John XXIII (1881–1963) epitomized the hope and idealism of the early 1960s. Kennedy was the first Roman Catholic elected to the US presidency, successfully overcoming the long-seated fear that a Catholic in the White House would be an agent of the Vatican. His youthful vigor and accessible wit, along with his dazzling wife, Jackie, and their adorable children, made Kennedy a hero to young people, who answered his call to service in great numbers in the Peace Corps and other volunteer agencies. Pope John, despite his advanced age, seemed as young as Kennedy, with his fresh ideas and ready smile. He wrote an encyclical on global peace, Peace on Earth (*Pacem in Terris,* April 11, 1963) and called for *aggiornamento* through a Council that would open the windows of the Church to the modern world.

These two charismatic figures gave young American Catholics a palpable sense of high expectations. Yes, it was possible to change the world and their generation would do it! Alas, the two Johns were rudely snatched away as their work was getting started. The collective mourning was deeply and personally felt.

Within this context, the Folk Mass can be seen as the American Catholic attempt to keep the fire of the early 1960s burning. The new generation had received its torch, determined to spread the idealistic light of their martyred president and beloved pope. John XXIII did not live to see the fruit of the Second Vatican Council (1962–1965) but its work continued, and Pope Paul VI (1897–1978) approved the groundbreaking *Constitution on the Sacred Liturgy* (*Sacrosanctum Concilium,* December 4, 1963). In the United States, the Latin Mass gave way to the new English liturgy one year later.

As these changes occurred, Ray Repp (b. 1942) and his guitar-strummed *Mass for Young Americans* captured the enthusiasm of the times and inspired young Catholics everywhere. For "one brief shining moment," as the musical *Camelot* so aptly put it, the Folk Mass became the soundtrack of American Catholic idealism, a dream shattered in 1968 with the three-fold impact of the assassinations of Robert Kennedy and Martin Luther King, Jr., and Pope Paul VI's encyclical, *Of Human Life* (*Humanae Vitae,* January 25, 1968).

For some observers, the Folk Mass was a failure, a well-intentioned but ultimately misguided attempt to marry the sacred with the secular. For others, it verified that the secular *was* the sacred, building on the foundation of the liturgical movement that began in the early twentieth century. The people's music seemed a good fit for the worship of the people of God. To fully appreciate the Folk Mass movement, one does well to hear and study the music within the context of its times.

As the 1960s faded into history, the Folk Mass became assimilated into the mainstream. But its legacy continues. The Folk Mass brought social justice themes into the liturgy and encouraged American Catholics to embrace congregational singing. The Folk Mass introduced the use of modern instrumentation and song styles in liturgy, planted the seeds for multicultural participation, and raised awareness in copyright justice. Lastly, the Catholic Folk Mass helped spark a similar movement in Protestant circles that eventually exploded as the multimillion dollar Contemporary Christian Music industry.

The fire still burns. This is the story of its kindling.

Chapter One
"Pange Lingua Gloriosi"

> Bowing his head over the bottle of Saint Emilion and a sliced loaf of whole-wheat bread on the living-room table, the priest prayerfully recalled the Last Supper: "And so we remember what Jesus said to his disciples, 'Take and eat, for this is my body.'" The consecration completed, the 24 men and women in the room kissed each other on the cheek or shook hands as a sign of peace. While a guitar plunked softly in the background, the worshippers shared the bread and wine and sang a hymn from the *Mass for Young Americans* by folk composer Ray Repp:
>
> > Sons of God, hear his Holy Word! Gather 'round the table of the Lord!
> > Eat his body, drink his blood, And we'll sing a song of love:
> > Allelu, allelu, allelu, alleluia![1]
>
> —*Time* magazine

So much changed so fast. On one Sunday in 1964, Catholics worshipped as they had for 400 years: in silence, on their knees, looking up to the altar at their priest as he prayed softly in Latin, his back to the congregation. The next week, this same priest faced the people, addressed them clearly in English, and even encouraged them to sing together. Accustomed to silence, American Catholics joined in song reluctantly, if at all. That, too, changed when young musicians brought their guitars and enthusiasm into the liturgy. Suddenly, the Church was rocking as Catholics discovered the unifying power of congregational singing.

But this was not an overnight sensation, nor was the Second Vatican Council the movement's progenitor. The "Guitar Mass," "Contemporary Mass," "Folk Mass" — whatever one wants to call it — is not exclusively the child of Vatican II. Such an assumption is a disservice to history.

The Folk Mass story begins neither with folk music nor with guitars, nor even with the Council. The Folk Mass had its origins in the Church's official music: Gregorian chant.

• ■ •

Dennis Fitzpatrick was 18 years old in 1955 when he entered Chicago's De Paul University to major in music composition. A recent graduate of the Christian Brothers School in Evanston, Illinois, Fitzpatrick was a tall, dark-haired young man with thick horn-rimmed glasses and a serious approach to music and life. Although he took up violin briefly at the age of five, he did not become passionate about music until his sophomore year of high school, when a recording of Bach's Cantata No. 4: *Christ lag in Todesbanden* (ca. 1707) literally changed his life. Dennis' stepfather, Dale Sandifur, a virtuoso pianist and French horn player, was more than happy to impart musical knowledge to the newly enthused convert. Young Dennis proved to be something of a prodigy, soaking up harmony, orchestration, counterpoint, and other complexities while becoming a pianist in his own right. Upon arriving at De Paul, his professors advanced him in the curriculum because of his impressive and masterful grasp of music theory.

Fitzpatrick sang baritone in the university chorus with Roger Nachtwey (1930–2007), a fellow student and teaching assistant whose interest was the liturgy. An engaging student with a dry wit, Nachtwey's enthusiasm for liturgy hooked Fitzpatrick, who soon incorporated organ and Gregorian chant into his course of studies. Among educated Catholics, this was a time of great excitement in anticipation of the new rites of Holy Week, promulgated by Pope Pius XII in his decree, *The Restoration of the Liturgy of Holy Week* (*Maxima Redemptionis*, November 19, 1955).

Nachtwey worked weekends as an organist, singer, and conductor at Sacred Heart Church in Hubbard Woods, a prosperous suburb of Chicago. At one point, Nachtwey searched for a substitute so he could attend an out-of-town conference. None of his De Paul classmates was available, and he bemoaned the prospect of canceling his plans. Upon hearing this, Fitzpatrick volunteered to substitute for his friend, despite having only a beginner's ability in Latin pronunciation. Nachtwey was reluctant at first, but within a few days Fitzpatrick played and sang the Latin chants like a pro. Nachtwey left for the conference and was confident that his liturgy was in good hands.

The pastor of Sacred Heart was immediately impressed with the talented young substitute and soon had both Nachtwey and Fitzpatrick on his payroll. The pastor was the legendary Monsignor Reynold Hillenbrand (1905–1979). This trio created a standard of excellence at Sacred Heart that made the parish a destination point for Catholics looking for cutting-edge liturgies.[2] A spark was kindled, although none of the trio could foresee the revolution in American liturgy that their heartfelt collaboration would bring about ten years later.

• ■ •

Reynold Henry Hillenbrand stands tall in an archdiocese already filled with such legendary giants as Cardinals Samuel Stritch (1887–1958), Albert Meyer (1903–1965), and John Cody (1907–1982). Historian Steven M. Avella refers to the years between 1940 and 1965 as the "era of confidence," when the Archdiocese of Chicago embraced massive institutional expansion, social justice activism, and liturgical innovation in a way that no other American diocese dared to attempt.

Msgr. Hillenbrand had a colorful and controversial career, and his influence was felt beyond the Chicago region through his equal passion for both liturgical reform and social justice activism. From 1936 through 1944, as rector of St. Mary of the Lake (now Mundelein) Seminary, he brought a fervor and zest for innovation that influenced generations of Chicago priests. Under Hillenbrand, the Dialogue Mass or *Missa Recitata*[3] became the seminary norm, as did the common recitation or chanting of the Divine Office.[4] His sermons were strictly based upon the readings of the Mass, an unheard of innovation at the time.

Hillenbrand frequently invited provocative speakers to address the seminarians, including Benedictine Father Virgil Michel (1890–1938), recognized founder of the American liturgical movement; Donald Attwater (1892–1977), editor of the liturgy magazine *Orate Fratres* (later renamed *Worship*); liturgical reformers Father H.A. Reinhold (1897–1968) and Monsignor Martin Hellriegel (1890–1981); Friendship House founder Catherine De Hueck Doherty (1896–1985); and, on one memorable occasion, Dorothy Day (1897–1980). He also took an active role in organizing the very first national Liturgical Week[5] in Chicago in 1940. He established regional liturgical conferences and workshops, and also found time to write for *Orate Fratres* magazine.

Because of Hillenbrand and the training he provided to priests and lay people, several other movements flourished in Chicago that had long-range influence around the country. There were the Pre-Cana and Cana conferences for marriage preparation, the Christian Family Movement, Specialized Catholic Action groups, and the successful social justice programs established by Hillenbrand's protégé, Monsignor Daniel Cantwell (1915–1996). With so many programs and involvements, it is no surprise that Hillenbrand's increasing absenteeism at the seminary came under scrutiny from both Cardinal Stritch and some adversaries on the seminary faculty.

In 1944, Hillenbrand became enmeshed in the Montgomery Ward labor strike, a dispute so volatile that President Franklin Roosevelt (1882–1945) sent the US army to intervene. Openly joining the picket line, even on behalf of a union he helped organize, was too much for Cardinal Stritch, who felt public controversy was abhorrent for his priests, especially the seminary rector. Stritch removed Hillenbrand from the seminary in July 1944 and "promoted" him to pastor of a suburban parish, perhaps hoping the distance from the city might cool down the priest's activist fire. The parishioners of Sacred Heart Parish in Winnetka were in for a wild ride from 1944 to 1974.[6]

Hillenbrand welcomed this opportunity to implement, on a parish level, the reforms in liturgy and social activism he taught at the seminary. He preached about liturgy from the pulpit, filled the parish library with the latest liturgical literature, began parish Catholic Action cells,[7] and pumped energy into the music program, all to facilitate the faithful's more active participation in the liturgy.

▪▪▪

To truly appreciate innovations occurring at Sacred Heart and later with the Folk Mass, it is important to understand the concept of Catholic liturgy before the 1964 changes brought about by the Second Vatican Council. Until then, Mass was celebrated in Latin, often referred to as "a dead language" understood by few and acknowledged only by lawyers, doctors, scientists, and the Catholic Church. Indeed, the Church had recognized Latin as its official liturgical language since the Council of Trent (1545–1563) had decreed that the Mass could only be celebrated in Latin.

In the pre-Council years, the priest "said" Mass and the people "heard" it. Only the priest and the "altar boys" performed any liturgical action, reciting the Latin prayers in a soft, barely audible tone. The priest, representing the people before God, turned his back to the congregation as they prayed together toward a large crucifix hung above the altar. The theology of the time taught Catholics a deep respect of the *mystery* of the Eucharist, as they joined the priest in the "unbloody sacrifice of Jesus on the cross." Catholics were taught a strong devotion to the Real Presence of Jesus in the Eucharist, demonstrated by their hushed reverence whenever they entered the church building.

As the priest managed the liturgical rites, the people "participated" by entering into a prayerful presence. When the Mass started, the congregation knelt in the pews and remained kneeling except for standing at the Gospel and sitting for the sermon and the offertory. It was considered good practice to bring a prayer book to read, or to pray the rosary while the priest said Mass. The more progressive participants followed the ritual with a personal missal.[8] There was no singing except at the designated "High Mass" when Gregorian chant was sung by a choir from the loft in the back of the church. For American Catholics, Sunday Mass was a quiet experience of spiritual reading or individual prayer. The only English they heard at liturgy was at the parish announcements, the sermon, and the prayers for the conversion of Russia at the conclusion of every Sunday Mass.

Liturgical critic Thomas Day makes the following observation:

> American Catholics not only accepted the idea of the Mass without a note of music, they boasted about it. This was their mark of distinction. It set them apart from their Protestant neighbors who went to church "only for music" and who had made music "the center of their worship." To a largely working-class Catholicism, music was the religion of the employers. The special attention paid to it in other denominations was a sign of their spiritual corruption. American Catholics, in contrast, had a higher and purer form of worship with a message so awesome that it could only be watched in silence and communicated through the most exalted symbols.[9]

Young people today marvel at the very idea of such a passive liturgy, but this was the only way that Catholics knew and, as such, they never complained. The Latin Mass was as integral to the American Catholic cultural experience as meatless Fridays, the May crowning of Mary, and rooting for the Notre Dame football team. As portrayed in the popular 1943 Bing Crosby movie *Going My Way,* this Catholic culture, along with the selfless dedication of parish priests and nuns, was a continuing source of reassurance and pride. For American Catholics, the prayerful and seemingly unchangeable silent Mass epitomized what their rock-solid faith was all about.

In 1952, Cardinal Stritch gave Msgr. Hillenbrand permission to experiment with the revised rites of the Easter Vigil, restored by Pius XII as an evening liturgy.[10] Hillenbrand's Sacred Heart parish sanctuary saw a major renovation in 1957 when the pastor turned the altar to face the people, years before Council reforms officially permitted this. It was around this time that Dennis Fitzpatrick and Roger Nachtwey became involved at Sacred Heart.

"We did as many kinds of experiments as we could within the rules because the Chancery office had people like Hillenbrand spied upon, in case they broke any rubrics in the liturgy," Nachtwey remembered. "Our people sang the refrains during the Communion procession, for instance. And, of course, Gelineau [psalmody] became famous back in the Fifties, and Monsignor liked that music. But we couldn't use any Gelineau Psalms [which were in English] except on weekdays when we had Low Masses with the kids. So he had one of the assistant priests, who was also a musician, write Latin texts for the Gelineau Psalms, so we could sing them in Latin at Sunday High Mass.[11]

"This is what got Dennis to compose. We would have a High Mass on Monday, Wednesday, and Friday during the week, at the children's school Mass. We sang everything in Latin the way it was supposed to be. And then on Tuesday and Thursday we had Low Mass. And, of course, in those days, you could sing anything you wanted in English [at Low Mass] and you could sing during the whole darn Mass if you wanted to and pay no attention to what was going on at the altar. But we devised music so that it was the same as at the High Mass so kids would know what they were singing."[12]

Fitzpatrick recalls, "I did my master's degree organ recital and choral conducting performance at Sacred Heart, at Msgr. Hillenbrand's church. We used to call him 'Hilly.' He had a terrible temper as a result of his car accident [in 1949]. But he was very kind to me, and when I asked him if I could play my recital there he said, 'Yes.' And then he asked me one day, did I think chant in English could work? I said, 'Oh, yes. Absolutely! Better than Latin. The reason is, people understood what they were doing.' And he said he was so relieved to hear that because that was a major topic of those days. Monsignor was as kind as he could be to me. He was just a wonderful man who encouraged me all the time."[13]

So Fitzpatrick and Nachtwey, with their pastor's blessing, had developed a clever way to legally sing the parts of the Mass in English by inserting newly composed chants in their corresponding places in the Latin Low Mass. Hillenbrand placed a high priority in liturgical training for his parish school, requiring the students to participate at Eucharist every morning at 10:00. The music directors welcomed this daily opportunity to refine their craft.

During Low Mass, as Hillenbrand recited the *"Sanctus,"* the children sang Fitzpatrick's "Holy, Holy, Holy" from his *English Mass Number One*, a respectful minor mode setting that echoed classic themes from Gregorian chant. When Monsignor recited the *"Agnus Dei,"* the students sang "Lamb of God." At High Mass they sang those same melodies but in the required Latin. The children of Sacred Heart made the connection and learned the meaning of those ancient words and how they fit with the liturgical action. Most importantly, they were no longer a passive audience, kneeling in the pews while watching the priest on the altar, but were one with their priest, praying with him the actual words of the liturgy in a way they could understand. In the 1950s, this was truly extraordinary.

---

1 "The Underground Church," *Time*, September 29, 1967

2 "As a case in point, my own experience as a visitor there during Holy Week in 1963: while it was my fortune to be a house guest of a friend in the parish, I learned that people coming from miles around had literally jammed hotels, motels, and trailer-park areas in the locality on the north shore of Lake Michigan above Chicago." From Devine, George, *Liturgical Renewal: An Agonizing Reappraisal* (Staten Island, NY: Alba House, 1973) 106.

3 Dialogue Mass was liturgy in which the whole assembly responded to the priest's prayers, rather than just the altar servers.

4 The Divine Office, now known as the Liturgy of the Hours, is a set of daily prayers prescribed by the Church to be recited at the canonical hours by the clergy, religious orders and, after Vatican II, the laity. It is based primarily on the chanting or recitation of the Psalms, supplemented by hymns and readings from the Bible and the writings of the early Church Fathers. It is the official public prayer of the Roman Catholic Church.

5 The national Liturgical Weeks were annual conferences originally sponsored by the Midwest Benedictine community. According to its bylaws, the goal of the Liturgical Week was to "lend our aid to the efforts of our hierarchy in arousing the Christian people to a deeper consciousness of their dignity as members of the Mystical Body of Christ." This goal was best expressed through active lay participation in the liturgy, and the Liturgical Weeks featured the finest cutting-edge speakers in the field. The first 1940 conference in Chicago had 1,200 in attendance; the 1964 conference in St. Louis welcomed more than 20,000 who were eager to participate in the first official English Mass. In the mid-1960s, the Liturgical Weeks became the regular forum of exposure for the Folk Mass composers.

6 For a fuller treatment on the life of Msgr. Reynold Hillenbrand see Steven M. Avella, *This Confident Church* (Notre Dame: University of Notre Dame Press, 1992) 30–42 and 151–186.

7 Catholic Action was an umbrella term for the "participation of the laity in the apostolate of the hierarchy," that is, the sanctification of souls. The movement was highly praised by Popes Pius XI and XII, and informed Vatican II by urging the laity to take seriously their vocation to Christianize the world. Small groups organized in "cells" would meet with a priest chaplain and use the "see-judge-act" method to bring "the whole program of the Divine Heart" to all aspects of life: the farms, the workplace, families, schools, and racial and social class struggle.

8 Missal, taken from *missa* (Latin for "Mass") is the name of the ritual book that was used for Catholic worship. There were two kinds of missals: an altar missal used by the priest (now called *Sacramentary for Mass*) and a personal missal used by the people in the pews. There was no standard personal missal in the pre-Vatican II days, although some, like the *St. Joseph Missal*, were more popular than others. All personal missals shared a bilingual presentation: The Latin text was followed by a loose, unofficial English translation, enabling the average Catholic to follow the liturgy. Personal missals were also filled with spiritual reading, devotional prayers, and religious art that the faithful could use for private reflection as the priest carried the burden of the ritual alone at the altar.

9 Day, Thomas, *Why Catholics Can't Sing* (Crossroad: New York: 1990) 9.

10 The restoration of the Easter Vigil was possibly the most popular of the liturgical reforms of Pope Pius XII. Previously, the Church celebrated the resurrection of Jesus only on Easter Sunday. Pius restored the ancient Vigil service that had been forgotten for many centuries. The new Vigil was celebrated at the proper evening hour in anticipation of Easter Sunday morning, with a reduced number of readings and the reintroduction of the rite of baptism as a living symbol of the Risen Christ.

11 Before Vatican II, there was distinction in solemnity between High Mass, where just about every major prayer was sung, and Low Mass, in which all the prayers were recited. Music at Low Mass was occasionally added more as an afterthought than in relation to the ritual.

12 Interview by author, March 6, 2004, by phone from Shawano, Wisconsin.

13 Interview by author, May 15, 2004, Las Vegas, Nevada.

Chapter Two
"Hang Down Your Head, Tom Dooley"

> I can't say when it occurred to me to write my own songs. I couldn't have come up with anything comparable or halfway close to the folk lyrics I was singing to define the way I felt about the world. I guess it happens to you by degrees. You just don't wake up one day and decide that you need to write songs, especially if you're a singer who has plenty of them and you're learning more every day. Opportunities may come along for you to convert something — something that exists into something that didn't yet. That might be the beginning of it.[1]
>
> —Bob Dylan

The Kingston Trio had somehow stolen the thunder from the rockers and pop crooners cranked out by commercial radio. Instead of raucous electric guitars or syrupy love lyrics, the young, clean-cut threesome played acoustic instruments and sang songs about condemned criminals, unrequited lovers, and soldiers going off to war. They took the folk music indigenous to America and presented it in a fresh way that captivated the record-buying public and, more specifically, the booming college-age crowd. In 1958, they made the murder ballad, "Tom Dooley," taught to them by Frank Proffitt (1913–1965), into their first hit single and helped to usher in a folk revival that took the country by storm.

One of the best things about this folk music was its accessibility. Anybody could take it up. All one needed was a guitar; no amplifiers or microphones were needed or even welcome. If you couldn't play the guitar you could simply throw your head back and sing along with everyone else. And what power there was in that group singing experience! The audience *became* the performers, entertaining themselves through their lively participation. Through folk music, the "fourth wall" of the stage was breached.

When "Tom Dooley" claimed the #1 spot on the Hit Parade, an explosion occurred. Record companies clamored to sign folk artists, each with their own repertory of ballads, blues, shanties, country tunes, work songs, protest songs, and more. Folk music, encompassing this variety, must have seemed like a cornucopia of sound, especially to the college-age listeners who had begun to tire of the repetitive three-chord rock'n'roll of their teen years.

Discerning fans noticed at concerts that folk artists often "covered" or performed the songs of other artists, even if it wasn't their own hit. Indeed, it appeared there was a tangible sense of community among the folk artists, with the Kingston Trio singing Pete Seeger's "Where Have All the Flowers Gone," or Peter, Paul, & Mary singing Bob

Dylan songs. Folk artists also had a way of taking old songs everybody knew from childhood and re-shaping them as their own, like Seeger did with "On Top of Old Smokey." Clearly, there was a common repertory of folk music that reached beyond the Tin Pan Alley school of commercial songwriting.

The folk song, like the Bible, grew from an oral tradition, pre-dating radio and recording technology. A singer observed a slice of life, turned the observation into a song and, with guitar or banjo, presented it to anyone who would hear, perhaps on a front porch, at the town square, or down in the mine. If people liked it they would sing along and bring the new song home to share with a new audience. Those audience members would in turn grow to love the song and take it to their homes to share with their family and friends. Sometimes the lyrics would change, sometimes the tune was modified, and no thought was ever given to composer credits or copyright protection. A song was a song, something free and sweet for the entire world to sing. And a good song was very sweet indeed.

Blanche Lemmon wrote, "American youth . . . are learning that this has always been a singing country and that songs of work, play, humor, lamentation, religion and love have dotted its progress throughout the years, poured forth spontaneously by its cowboys, its searchers for gold, its cotton pickers, its sailors, lumberjacks, farmers, teamsters, mountaineers, railroaders and others, each in characteristic style."[2]

As the Industrial Revolution transformed society and shifted the focus of enterprise from the farm to the cities, there arose an interest in the folk music of rural America. Inspired by similar efforts in Great Britain, music scholars began the slow and arduous task of collecting folk songs with the crude recording technology of the period. Most notable were the efforts of John Avery Lomax (1867–1948), a songbook publisher who, on behalf of the Library of Congress, went on a music collecting tour across the Deep South with his teenage sons in 1932. With a cumbersome recording machine hauled in the back of their car, the Lomaxes interviewed local singers and recorded their songs. They discovered a wealth of traditional songs and original, topical material that was eloquent in commenting on the struggles of the Depression era.

John Lomax's publication of newfound folksongs led to an explosion of interest among the public. His influential songbooks included *American Ballads and Folk Songs* (1934), *Negro Folk Songs as Sung by Lead Belly* (1936), *Our Singing Country* (1941), and *Folk Song: USA* (1947), all compiled and published with his son Alan (1915–2002). The folksongs that previously had only the slow-but-sure medium of oral transmission became popularized on a grander scale through these and other songbooks.

This traditional folk music took root in the cities as a medium of radical thought. Topical songs of protest and lament had been around as early as the 1800s, but they began to flourish in the early twentieth century as labor activists began to see folk music's power and potential in educating and uniting people for their causes. Rallies organized by leftist organizations often began with a folk singer who warmed up the crowd by singing well-known songs rewritten with pro-union lyrics. It was within this liberal milieu that the folksong movement flourished, epitomized by the dynamic performances and recordings of artists like Woody Guthrie (1912–1967), Burl Ives (1909–1995), Pete Seeger (b. 1919), and the Weavers. Vibrant troubadours who caught the fancy of a growing left-wing movement, their singing of the traditional folk repertoire was placed within the context of the burning issues of the day: rights for the workers, social equality, and the struggle for civil rights. In time, their originally composed songs went beyond the subtle textures of the traditional folksongs and directly challenged the establishment.

By the late 1940s that "establishment" could no longer ignore the liberal folksong movement. The celebrative victory of World War II soon gave way to an anti-Communist paranoia led by Senator Joseph McCarthy (1908–1957), under whose influence the House Committee on Un-American Activities blacklisted artists across all entertainment fields. Careers were destroyed and lives ruined as left-leaning artists suddenly found themselves branded as part of the Communist threat to the security of the nation. Under this high-profile glare, singers like Ives, who was a willing witness for the committee, abandoned their liberal songlists and began performing less threatening fare. For others, there was simply no way to get work as a performer. Pete Seeger was forced to stop performing for a time.

As the 1950s unfolded, bringing its suburban post-war prosperity, America seemed to settle into a comfortable conformity, even as the Cold War and racial unrest escalated. Elvis Presley (1935–1977) and his rock'n'roll contemporaries made a splash with teenagers, much to the dismay of their parents. Within this context, folk music's second wave began.

The Kingston Trio-style of folk music was stripped of any left-wing associations. Indeed, by the time "Tom Dooley" was released, such links were conveniently forgotten and pushed into the closet. Folksinger/photographer John Cohen (b. 1932) wrote in 1959: "The emphasis is no longer on social reform or on world-wide reform. The effort is focused more on a search for real and human values."[3]

The impact of the Kingston Trio cannot be overstated. Their clean-cut style was and still is decried by folk purists who insist that the group's "collegiate" interpretations did not represent folk music in all its diversity and integrity. Still, there's no denying that without the Kingston Trio's popularization, folk music would never have re-entered American culture in a way that eventually blossomed into the protest-laden radicalism of the next decade. The teenagers who embraced the Trio in the 1950s became the movers and shakers of the 1960s.

"Now don't get me wrong," said one Southern California enthusiast. "We're typical teens and like rock'n'roll, but you have interested us in a new type of music. And as my mother says, 'the Kingston Trio records teach you something about people that you wouldn't ever have a chance to meet' (such as zombies).... Thanks ever so much for introducing a new world of music to us."[4]

The stage was set for Catholic composers such as Ray Repp (b. 1942), Paul Quinlan

(b. 1939), Germaine Habjan (b. 1944), Carey Landry (b. 1944), Gary Ault (b. 1944), Jack Miffleton (b. 1942), and a host of other future Folk Mass composers who embraced the new, clean, folk music as their own. Not so coincidentally, most, if not all, of these early Folk Mass pioneers were in the seminary or part of a religious community.

▪▪▪

Ray Repp was born in St. Louis, the oldest of nine children of Rita and Walter Repp. A convert to Catholicism, Walter's devotion became a hallmark for the family, who often knelt together in their living room to pray the rosary. The Repp children all attended Catholic schools and colleges. Yet, despite their devotion, Ray's parents were not encouraging when he told them of his desire to enter the seminary right after eighth grade. Inspired by the priests who served in his parish, the young boy wanted to join the Servite Order whose minor seminary was in Chicago, quite a distance from home. Ray's parents had no support for his Servite plans. However, a compromise was reached when they allowed their son to enter the diocesan preparatory seminary in St. Louis.

Ray persevered through high school and entered St. Louis' Cardinal Glennon College Seminary at the height of the Kingston Trio's popularity. A slender young man with short-cropped, dark hair and a ready smile, Repp was filled with youthful idealism. The seminary took him out of the world to attain his goal of the priesthood without distractions but, like other young people of the era, he found the new folk music irresistible. He soon bought his own guitar — a Gibson — and devoted much time to learning how to play it, picking up valuable cues by listening to his favorite folk records.

As part of his studies, Repp attended a class on the Book of Psalms taught by Vincentian Father Bruce Vawter (d. 1986), the distinguished professor of Scripture at Cardinal Glennon College Seminary. Repp learned the poetry of the Psalms and their themes of praise and lament. He studied their *sitz im leben*, i.e., the life situations in which they were composed, and how each expressed the very real emotions of the psalmist. Most impressively, the young seminarian discovered the Psalms were meant to be sung, accompanied by a stringed instrument, no less!

It wasn't long before Repp made a connection between the ancient psalms and modern folk music. Finding a place to be alone, he paged through his study Bible and came upon Psalm 117 in its two-verse entirety:

> Praise the Lord, all nations. Extol him, all you peoples!
> For his love is strong, the Lord's faithfulness eternal. Alleluia!

He played the guitar chords he had learned and wondered how the Kingston Trio might sing this Psalm. Finding a comfortable beat and a chord sequence, he decided to express the Psalm in a new way:

Praise to the Lord for he is good, all nations.
Join we now in the love of the Lord forevermore!

© 1966, Otter Creek Music. Published by OCP. All rights reserved.

This was no Top 40 hit, but "Forevermore," as it was titled, was certainly catchy and Ray was pleased with his effort. He also wondered what he would do with it. Who would want to hear a Psalm when everyone was singing popular songs like "M.T.A," "Greenback Dollar," and "This Land Is Your Land"? He folded the handwritten songsheet into his pocket and went on with his day. Soon it would be time for night prayer and, in the morning, the seminarians would rise and pray the Latin Mass together. It was 1962 and the Second Vatican Council was just getting started.

---

1 Bob Dylan, *Chronicles, Volume One* (New York: Simon & Schuster, 2004) 51.
2 Blanche Lemmon, "American Folk Songs," *Etude 58* (April 1940), 220. As quoted in Ronald D. Cohen, *Rainbow Quest: The Folk Music Revival and American Society, 1940–1970* (Amherst and Boston: University of Massachusetts Press, 2002) 8.
3 As quoted in Cantwell, Robert, *When We Were Good: The Folk Revival* (Cambridge and London: Harvard University Press, 1996) 22.
4 Unnamed folk music fan, as quoted in Ronald D. Cohen, *Rainbow Quest: The Folk Music Revival and American Society, 1940–1970* (Amherst and Boston: University of Massachusetts Press, 2002) 133.

Chapter Three
"Veni, Creator Spiritus"

According to Pope John, it was toward the end of 1958, shortly after assuming the papacy, that he engaged the late Cardinal Tardini in a troubled conversation regarding the state of the world and the Church's role in it. Noting the agitation and anxiety in which the modern world was plunged, and the apparently hopeless repetition of clamorings for peace and justice, he asked his Secretary of State what might be done to give the world an example of peace and concord between men and an occasion for new hope, when suddenly there sprang to his own lips the words, "A Council!" Uncertain of his most intimate aide's reaction to such an idea, and expecting to be deluged with a torrent of objections from this seasoned statesman, the pope was overcome when Cardinal Tardini responded with an immediate and emotion-charged assent: *"Si, si! Un Concilio!"*[1]

Pope John XXIII (1958–1963) captivated the whole world with his charm and folksy informality, so refreshing after the years of stoic aloofness emanating from his predecessor, Pius XII (1939–1958). Stories circulated about how he delighted infirm children during unprecedented pastoral visits to Roman hospitals; of how he visited a local prison and gave hope to an inmate wondering if God still loved him; of how he worked the room after his formal audiences, greeting friends and acquaintances with unabashed joy, much to the annoyance of his handlers; of how, after carefully rehearsing the protocol of addressing the visiting First Lady of the United States, he extended his huge arms and simply exclaimed, "Jacqueline!" as she entered the papal chamber.

Such stories instantly endeared this pope to Catholics and non-Catholics alike. Nevertheless, his call to invoke a council was surprising. It would be the first large-scale gathering of the world's bishops since 1869. The interrupted First Vatican Council (1869–1870) left much unfinished business, managing only to define the doctrine of papal infallibility. The Second Vatican Council's agenda was encapsulated by the Holy Father himself in an Italian word that became a catch phrase for the 1960s Church: *aggiornamento,* or "bringing up to date."

The Second Vatican Council eventually promulgated sixteen major documents, all with far-reaching implications. Among these were the Dogmatic Constitution on the Church (*Lumen Gentium*, 1964), the Dogmatic Constitution on Divine Revelation (*Dei Verbum*, 1965), the Decree on Ecumenism (*Unitatis Redintegratio*, 1964), the Decree on the Media of Social Communications (*Inter Mirifica*, 1963), and the Pastoral Constitution on the Church in the Modern World (*Gaudium et Spes*, 1965). When Pope John XXIII died on June 3, 1963, in the midst of the Council's deliberations, his work was continued under the capable hands of his successor, Paul VI. Pope John XXIII did, however, preside over the lively discussions on a topic that the bishops unanimously selected as their initial document: the Constitution on the Sacred Liturgy (*Sacrosanctum Concilium*, 1963).

Almost a half-century later, the Second Vatican Council has become an historical event, akin to an ancient war. Only a handful of the participating bishops, theologians, *periti*, and observers are still alive, and their numbers dwindle every year. Catholic students may learn about the Council in their religion classes but its work has become as distant as World War II. Some older adults may recall the excitement the Council stirred in the Church of their youth, but would be hard pressed to provide an account of its contributions. The legacy of Vatican II is found in the Council's documents, remarkable gems unfortunately written in a technical jargon understood only by professional ecclesiastics.

Revelation, ecumenism, and the role of the Church in the world are important concepts that a thoughtful Catholic may appreciate, but may have questionable relevance to everyday life. It was in the liturgy, celebrated daily and attended weekly by the faithful, that the effects of the Council truly came home. Today's youth may never fully comprehend the emotional upheaval their grandparents and parents experienced when, on the First Sunday of Advent in 1964, the typical parish's Latin Mass suddenly became a thing of the past. To understand the context of this breakthrough, there is another remarkable contemporary of Pope John XXIII to consider.

There was a Catholic in the White House! John Fitzgerald Kennedy (1917–1963), the junior senator from Massachusetts, had successfully overcome lingering anti-Catholic sentiment in predominantly Protestant America through a masterful campaign mixing principle, reassurance, and personal charisma. For American Catholics, Kennedy's election was a breakthrough that symbolized the growing influence of their faith in the nation and in the world.

The time was right for a Catholic president. When Catholic Al Smith (1873–1944) ran for the office in 1928, roughly 16% of the country was Catholic and the majority of them were poor and uneducated immigrants. Critics played on then-common prejudices, claiming that if Smith won he would take orders directly from Rome. In the forty years since the 1928 election, the Catholic population had grown four-fold and represented all economic strata. The Catholic vote may not have tipped the close election in Kennedy's favor, but clearly the anti-Catholic vote was no longer a factor.

The early 1960s was a time of bright promise. Kennedy was only 43 when he entered office, and his young family captured the nation's imagination. The daily newspapers regularly featured front-page photos of the president playing with his toddler son "John-John" and his pre-school daughter Carolyn. On February, 14, 1962, Jackie Kennedy welcomed Americans into the White House in a ratings-busting television special that showcased her tasteful yet historical restoration of many rooms in the presidential mansion. Jack and Jackie Kennedy were a handsome and glamorous couple regaling the world's leaders and artists with style and charm.

As his famous January 20, 1961, inaugural address demonstrated, Kennedy was big on vision but cautious in action. Kennedy jump-started one of humanity's grandest adventures with his promise to put a man on the moon, and he rallied tens of thousands of young people to serve in the Peace Corps. But he also escalated the country's military presence in Vietnam and moved slowly on civil rights. Sadly, an assassin's bullet cut down President Kennedy on November 22, 1963, just as he was maturing in office. We will never know how events may have unfolded had he lived, but his vision, optimism, and youthful vigor are forever etched in a generation's collective memory.

American Catholics took pride in their "two Johns," who seemed to share a vision of optimism and peace. Shortly before the opening session of the Council, Kennedy sent Pope John XXIII a special message:

> In the face of staggering problems which, from the human point of view, seem at times to be almost insoluble, people all over the world have found reason for renewed confidence and courage in the welcome thought that the Fathers of the Council, as Your Holiness indicated in your Radio Message of September 11, will give special attention to the grave economic and social problems which daily press upon suffering humanity in almost all parts of the world but, more particularly, in the economically underdeveloped nations. It is very heartening to know that the Council, in the words of Your Holiness, will strive to deepen the fellowship and love which are "the natural needs of man" and "are imposed on the Christian as rules for his relationship between man and man, and between people and people." We hope that the Council will be able to present in clear and persuasive language effective solutions to the many problems confronting all of us and, more specifically, that its decisions will significantly advance the cause of international peace and understanding.[2]

Councils never occur in a vacuum but rather reflect the current needs and concerns of the Church. Immediately after Pope John XXIII announced on January 25, 1959, that he was going to convene the Council, an extraordinary preparation period commenced as the best and brightest minds in the Church expended passionate energy to gather, collate, and synthesize agenda topics from bishops and theologians around the world.

> In preparing for the Council, Pope John kept an invisible but firm hand on the 800 theologians and experts who were called to Rome to prepare the agenda. In less than three years, they sifted and codified a mountain of facts relating to ecclesiastical affairs in the modern world, covering everything from the rigid norms of canon law to the price of beeswax in Nigeria.[3]

In preparing for the document on the liturgy, the theologians drew on the efforts of liturgical reform and experimentation that, although unknown to most Catholics, had begun decades before the Council's opening session.

The beginning of the modern liturgical movement is generally agreed to have occurred in 1832, when Benedictine Dom Prosper Louis Pascal Guéranger (1805–1875) sought and received permission from Pope Gregory XVI (1831–1846) to reestablish the ancient monastery at Solesmes, France, as a liturgical center. This effort was a reaction to the chaos of liturgical innovation that had grown in the leaderless Church of post-revolutionary France. Guéranger worked to standardize the liturgy by focusing on a strict interpretation of the Roman rite in celebrations of the Eucharist and the Divine Office and promoting the return to Gregorian chant as the official music of the Church. Through his efforts, the monastery at Solesmes became renowned for the beauty and authenticity of its chant realizations, a reputation it enjoys to this day.

The reform movement spread throughout continental Europe and especially in Belgium, where Dom Lambert Beauduin (1873–1960) took up Guéranger's mantle as head of the movement. Beauduin's most notable contribution was the publication of his paper *La vraie priere de l'Egise* delivered in 1909 at the National Congress of Catholic Works in Malines, Belgium. In this document, Beauduin called for the "full and active participation of all people in the Church's life and ministry, particularly in the liturgy," fifty-four years before Vatican II used similar language in the *Constitution on the Sacred Liturgy*. Beauduin took his inspiration for this call from Pope Pius X (1903–1914), who encouraged the active participation of the faithful in his 1903 proclamation, *Tra le sollecitudini*.[4]

In the United States, the liturgical movement grew through the efforts of a young Benedictine, Virgil Michel, who was sent in 1924 to study in Rome under Dom Beauduin. Michel developed a passion for liturgy and dedicated his life to increasing the faith and liturgical devotion of the faithful. He continued his studies at the Catholic University at Louvain, learning first-hand of the great work of the Belgian liturgical centers.

Michel returned home to St. John's Abbey in Collegeville, Minnesota, with a convert's zeal that immediately impacted the American Catholic Church. He was a guest lecturer at St. Mary of the Lake (Mundelein) Seminary during Monsignor Hillenbrand's tenure as rector. An advisor to Baroness Catherine DeHueck, Dorothy Day, and other social justice reformers, Michel was one of the first theologians to connect the burgeoning social justice movement with the liturgy, a correlation later validated by Pius XII's 1943 encyclical, *Mystici Corporis Christi*.

There were other liturgical reformers in America. In 1946, Monsignor Joseph P. Morrison (1894–1957) helped found the Vernacular Society, a lay organization dedicated to the promulgation of English in the Roman liturgy. With the colorful Lt. Colonel K. John Ross-Duggan (1888–1967) as secretary, the Vernacular Society held annual meetings (often during the national Liturgical Weeks), published a journal called *Amen,* and lobbied aggressively for the vernacular with the American bishops and with Rome. They scored a victory of sorts in 1954 when the Sacred Congregation of Rites approved the use of English for certain sacraments in the official Ritual book.[5]

∙■∙

The daily sessions of the Council went from about quarter to ten in the morning until quarter past twelve in the afternoon. In the afternoon, various committees and groups analyzed what had been said in the morning session.[6]

All the Council sessions were conducted in Latin, without simultaneous translation. United Nations-style interpreters had been ruled out because of the fear of electronic leakage to the media. Thus the European bishops had a linguistic advantage over their American counterparts, whose fluency in Latin had been lost in the years since their long-ago seminary days. This situation gave the greater importance to the smaller afternoon meetings and to the evening meals taken informally throughout Rome. These became the true forum of discussion among the Council Fathers as they debated the daily issues with bishops both from their own countries and from around the world. This nightly personal give-and-take on the Council agenda enabled the bishops to be better informed when they voted on the issues the following morning.

Meanwhile, half a world away, a dedicated group of lay people was conspiring to influence the direction of the Council's discussion on the liturgy.

∙■∙

Mary Sandifur (Fitzpatrick) was always there for her son. A leading soprano with opera companies in San Francisco, Oakland, and New York, she was delighted when her son Dennis chose to study music at De Paul University. He was seven when his father died and Mary took on the challenge of raising the family while working as a musician. And nineteen years later, she was supporting Dennis by cooking up a delicious feast to feed the small band of people who had turned her immaculately kept home into a chaotic shipping department. It was July 21, 1963, and the young composer chose to celebrate his 26th birthday with a work party.

A new session of the Council would commence that fall. The work party was preparing to ship the *Demonstration English Mass* long-play record and altar missal to the 500 English-speaking bishops returning to Rome. Composed, recorded, and edited by Fitzpatrick with assistance from the faithful Roger Nachtwey, *Demonstration English Mass* was the first completely realized vernacular liturgy, with the entire Mass sung in English from the opening Sign of the Cross to the concluding *Ite, Missa est*. Fitzpatrick's efforts were recognized by the press:

> Mr. Fitzpatrick's new recording will prove a bombshell. It presents what he modestly calls a *Demonstration English Mass,* in which the entire Mass is sung to a fresh, chant-like musical setting. It must be heard to be believed. Here we have a real congregation (a volunteer one, of course), which rehearsed for only a half-hour to make the recording, joyously singing out the Mass in words that are totally understood. All is sheer gain; no loss of dignity or reverence; the mystery remains, but not the mystification.[7]

The expense of recording, printing, and mailing this landmark project was underwritten by three couples who pledged a total investment of $10,000: Mr. and Mrs. Dale Sandifur, Fitzpatrick's mother and stepfather; Mr. and Mrs. John L. Kellogg, Fitzpatrick's brother-in-law and an heir to the Battle Creek, Michigan, cereal company; and Mr. and Mrs. Albert G. Degen, Kellogg's mother and father-in-law. Fitzpatrick called them the "Friends of the English Liturgy" and invited others to join the cause of effecting the vernacular changeover of the Roman rite. The group was the foundation for what eventually became known as FEL Publications.

Demonstration English Mass (*DEM*) was never intended to be only a recording or a performance piece. From the onset, Fitzpatrick's goal was to demonstrate how beautiful the liturgy could be in English, with music especially composed to encourage congregational participation. After several years of experimentation at Sacred Heart Parish with Msgr. Hillenbrand, Fitzpatrick knew that chant would work in English, and he staged a full, although unofficial, Mass to prove it.

In just a few short months, *DEM* became a sensation, playing to packed halls at seminaries and universities throughout the Chicago region, many of them ecumenical. The largest *Demonstration English Mass* was given for 1,500 overflowing participants at Rockefeller Memorial Chapel at the University of Chicago. Northwestern University also sponsored a demonstration Mass in Alice Millar Chapel.

It looked like a Mass and felt like a Mass, but the fully vested "celebrant" was not an ordained priest. Roger Nachtwey often played this role, and his performance was so convincing that Fitzpatrick jokingly warned his friend to make the homily less appealing so people wouldn't think it was a real Mass.

In 1961, the *Demonstration English Mass* could hardly be mistaken for a genuine liturgy. The full enthusiastic participation by the assembly, in English, was a far cry from the silent Latin Mass currently celebrated in the parishes. It was an exciting preview of what the Mass would soon become.

DEM also introduced some startling innovations that were years ahead of their time: the Prayer of the Faithful (called the "Bidding Prayers"); the Sign of Peace; and, most radical of all, a completely English-sung Canon (now known as Eucharistic Prayer I). Nachtwey, a Latin expert, rendered the English translation, the chant was entirely Fitzpatrick's work, and most of the *DEM*'s rubrical ideas were taken from the work of Msgr. H.A. Reinhold, whose influential book, *Bringing the Mass to the People* (Baltimore, MD: Helicon Press, 1960), proved to be remarkably prescient, providing ideas later adopted during the reform of the Roman rite. Reinhold himself attended a *Demonstration English Mass* during a Liturgical Week conference and met Fitzpatrick, informing the composer of his great pleasure in seeing so many of his ideas realized in such a tangible manner.

DEM's popularity in seminaries caught the attention of the Chicago Chancery staff and Fitzpatrick was called to visit Cardinal Albert Meyer (1903–1965), who expressed his concern only in the vaguest of terms. He exhorted the composer to clear things first with Monsignor Charles N. Meter (1911–1998), head of the archdiocesan liturgical commission. Meter's desire was to control the burgeoning movement by requiring Fitzpatrick to seek permission before booking another *DEM*. Fitzpatrick listened politely to the Chancery officials, then went ahead and continued his liturgies. This rather headstrong determination would become a hallmark of Fitzpatrick's personal and professional vision.

For example, Fitzpatrick was also president of the Chicago-based Pius XII Society, formed when Cardinal Stritch (Meyer's predecessor) banned the Vernacular Society in the archdiocese. Fitzpatrick re-organized the forbidden group and diverted ecclesial suspicion by cleverly renaming it in honor of the long-reigning pope.

Dennis Fitzpatrick was a logical choice for president and he relished the role. Assisted by Roger Nachtwey, they turned the society's monthly newsletter into a primary source of information on the Council deliberations. Simple and unpretentiously printed in mimeograph format, this newsletter was a lifeline that kept progressives informed of the latest news of liturgical reform. It was filled with generous quotes from papal liturgical documents, tips on how to conduct a Dialogue Mass or Bible Vigil, examples of the music notation for English chant, up-to-the-minute reports from the Council, and unabashed promotion of Fitzpatrick's *Demonstration English Mass*. In short, this newsletter was the pulse of the vernacular movement in Chicago. In the December 1962 edition, Fitzpatrick wrote:

> Although the Council sessions are in secret, the frankness of the Fathers outside of the Council and the reports of disagreement among the prelates in Council concerning the use of vernacular by the Vatican press office are refreshing and a source of comfort to many of us laymen. It is a sign of vitality and deep-felt concern that there should be honest disagreement about the use of Latin vs. the Vernacular.
>
> Interest in the vernacular means interest in participation at Mass. Both laymen and priests concern themselves with this problem because of their respective roles. A layman realizes that if he is to possess the true Christian spirit, "the first and indispensable source" of this spirit is participation in the liturgy and, inasmuch as the use of Latin is a barrier to this participation, he concerns himself with the use of the vernacular....
>
> Obviously, then, having the liturgy in a language we can understand so that we can intelligently participate in the services is a basic issue.... Let us hope then, now that the question of the vernacular is in the minds and thoughts of our bishops, that frank discussions will be followed by effective implementations.[8]

The Kennedy era of bright promise was in full swing as the Council Fathers began their work on the document on the liturgy. Change was tangibly around the corner, and Fitzpatrick and other progressives confidently kept the fires burning on the home front. There was never a more exciting or hopeful time for liturgical reform.

1. Rynne, Xavier, *Vatican Council II* (Maryknoll, New York: Farrar, Orbis Books, 1999) 3. Rynne was the pen name of Redemptorist Father Francis X. Murphy (1914–2002). Murphy's middle name was Xavier and his mother's birth name was Rynne.
2. Kennedy, John F., *Message to Pope John XXIII on the Occasion of the Opening of the Second Vatican Council,* Dated September 27, 1962. and released October 5, 1962
3. Rynne, Xavier, *Vatican Council II* (Maryknoll, New York: Farrar, Orbis Books, 1999) 8.
4. Pecklers, Keith F., *The Unread Vision: The Liturgical Movement in the United States of America: 1926–1955* (Collegeville, MN: Liturgical Press, 1998) 2.
5. For a fuller treatment of the Vernacular Society see Keith F. Pecklers, *The Unread Vision: The Liturgical Movement in the United States of America: 1926–1955* (Collegeville, MN: Liturgical Press, 1998) 63–66.
6. From a personal account by Bishop Myles McKeon of Australia, from Prendergast, Michael and Ridge, M.D., editors, *Voices from the Council* (Portland, OR: Pastoral Press, 2004) 71.
7. McNaspy, C.J., *America* magazine, August 10, 1963.
8. *Pius XII Society Newsletter,* December 1962.

Chapter Four
"God Is Love"

> I saw the rapport of the bishops. They asked profound questions and openly dialogued. We saw bishops truly going through a change in thinking. You know, John Tracy Ellis, prior to Vatican II, asked the American bishops what they expected from Vatican II. ...and for the most part it was only to be a tinkering with canon law. No one was thinking big about Scripture and tradition, ecumenism or thinking about vernacular liturgy or reform of the liturgy.... They went through a real change of heart that could have only been effected by the Spirit. The American bishops did go through a real renewal and then were in the forefront of issues like religious freedom. As we know, all the Council Fathers except four signed the Constitution on the Sacred Liturgy.[1]
>
> —Bishop Donald W. Trautman

One year after the Council opened, the bishops reconvened for the beginning of the second session on September 29, 1963. Happily, the new pope, Paul VI, pledged to continue the work begun by his predecessor. On this first evening of the second session, some English-speaking bishops met for cocktails at the North American College in Vatican City, reacquainting themselves with friends they had not seen in a year. Amid the clinking of glasses and friendly banter, music could be heard from a record player. It seemed to be Gregorian chant, a sound not so unusual in the Vatican. But several bishops drew closer to listen more attentively when they realized the chant was in English. It was the *Demonstration English Mass* by Dennis Fitzpatrick.

The following news excerpt reveals Fitzpatrick's influence on the contentious American hierarchy, who received the July 1963 mailing of the Friends of the English Liturgy (FEL).[2]

> VATICAN CITY — The first American High Mass, in English, written by a Chicago composer, is almost sure to be included in the clearance of vernacular liturgy by the Vatican Council. But unless a majority of the sharply divided American bishops approve the experiment, its full realization in all American churches may be postponed for years. The final approval is up to the 280 American bishops and abbots, 170 of them still in Rome.
>
> The history-making Mass, acclaimed by both Catholic and Protestant liberals, is by Dennis Fitzpatrick of Chicago, a young composer trained at De Paul University.... "Fitzpatrick's name deserves to be known

everywhere," said San Francisco's Episcopalian bishop James A. Pike, who called the Mass "an exciting, great achievement." Not all the American Cardinals agree. At the extremes of opposition stand the conservative Francis Cardinal Spellman of New York and James Francis Cardinal McIntyre of Los Angeles. Cardinal Spellman has been quoted as saying: "As long as I am alive a vernacular Mass will never be sung in my archdiocese." The only Cardinal among the traditionally cautious American episcopacy prepared to favor openly the Chicago Mass is Joseph Cardinal Ritter of St. Louis, who has even tested it before his priests. The Midwestern liberal said he found "much pleasure" in listening to the Mass sung on a record. "It gave us all some idea how the vernacular may be used to great advantage. Many of our priests were favorably impressed." Chicago's own Albert Gregory Cardinal Meyer gave word through a spokesman at Chicago House that "judgment now would be premature."[3]

Cardinals McIntyre (1886–1979) and Spellman (1889–1967) represented a traditional viewpoint that became lost in the increasingly progressive sweep of the Council. For example, toward the end of a rather lengthy discussion on the *Constitution on the Sacred Liturgy,* after the bishops of Africa and Asia had given powerful arguments for the adaptation of the liturgy to the social, intellectual, and natural environment of their people, McIntyre presented an intervention in shaky Latin that amazed and confounded his peers: "Active participation of the faithful at Mass is nothing but a distraction."[4]

> What further dismayed a large number of the bishops was the fact that since the statement was made so late in the debate, it showed that the Cardinal of Los Angeles had paid little attention to the heart of the discussion which turned around the mysteries of faith as they were to be made actual in the lives of both priests and faithful through the liturgy.[5]

The Cardinal of New York did not fare too well himself, despite his standing as a rotating president-moderator of the sessions.

> Cardinal Spellman appeared also to have been poorly advised. When these two American prelates who, while vigorous in defense of the retention of Latin in the Mass, came out, contrary to all expectations, in favor of the clergy being allowed to read their breviaries in English, an Italian archbishop was compelled to exclaim: "*Ah! Questi Americani!* Now they want the priest to pray in English and the people to pray in Latin!"[6]

McIntyre and Spellman returned home to a Church that would soon break out into the modern world, despite their best efforts to contain it or deny it.

When Pope Paul VI promulgated the *Constitution on the Sacred Liturgy*[7] on December 4, 1963, Americans were still reeling from the shocking death of their charismatic President Kennedy only weeks before. The Singing Nun's folksy "Dominique" was the #1 hit song on the radio at this time, her lilting voice and solo guitar a soothing balm and harbinger of the liturgical changes to come.[8] The American bishops decided to implement the Council's first document immediately, designating the First Sunday of Advent, November 29, 1964, as the starting date for the new English Mass. The mad scramble was on!

As outlined in the following chart, the newly approved liturgy was a transitional and confusing hybrid of English and Latin.

Pre-Vatican II (All recited by the priest in Latin, except where noted)	First Sunday of Advent (November 29, 1964)
Prayers at the Foot of the Altar	Entrance Song (Sung in English by the congregation)
Introit	Prayers at the Foot of the Altar (Recited in English by the congregation and priest; omitted if an Entrance Song is sung)
Kyrie Eleison	Lord, Have Mercy (Recited in English by the congregation and priest)
Gloria	Glory to God (Recited in English by the congregation and priest)
Collect	Opening Prayer (Recited in Latin by the priest)
Epistle	Epistle (Read in English by a lay reader)
Gradual	Meditation Song (Recited/sung in English by the congregation)
Gospel	Gospel (Read in English by the priest)
Sermon (in English by priest)	Homily (Preached in English by the priest)
Credo	Creed (Recited in English by the congregation only on Sundays and great feasts)
Offertory Prayer	Offertory Song (Sung in English by the congregation)
Secret	Prayer Over the Gifts (Recited in Latin by the priest)
Preface	Preface (Recited in Latin by the priest and the congregation)
Sanctus	Holy, Holy (Recited in English by the priest and the congregation)
Canon	Canon (Recited in Latin by the priest)
Pater Noster	Lord's Prayer (Recited in English by the priest and the congregation)
Libera Nos	Fraction Rite (Recited in Latin by the priest)
Pax Domini	Prayer for Peace (Recited in Latin by the priest and the congregation)
Angus Dei	Lamb of God (Recited in English by the congregation)
Domine Non Sum Dignus	Lord, I Am Not Worthy (Recited in English by the congregation)
Communion	Communion Rite (English, priest and congregation)
Communion Prayer	Communion Song (Sung in English by the congregation)
Ite, Missa Est and Blessing Last Gospel	Dismissal and Blessing (Recited in English by the priest and the congregation)
Prayers for the Conversion of Russia (by priest and congregation in English)	Closing Hymn (Optional) (Sung in English by the congregation)

Why a bilingual liturgy? Why not an entire English Mass as the reformers advocated? Conciliar compromise was part of the reason, as was the speed of the reform. The American bishops had less than twelve months to come up with new English texts after Pope Paul VI approved the *Constitution on the Sacred Liturgy*. It would take years to compose worthy English texts for the entire Mass, texts that would need to be approved by the American bishops and, ultimately, the Vatican. Until this approval process was complete, Rome allowed for the national bishops conferences to use transitional, experimental translations so Catholics could experience the reforms of the Council without delay. The hope was that these interim translations would serve to help polish a more refined translation down the road.[9]

There was also the shock value to consider. It was assumed that Americans, accustomed to an unchanging worship, would need a transitional English-Latin liturgy to ease them into a change considered unthinkable only five years earlier. To assist the faithful in understanding the reform, the US Bishops' Commission on the Liturgical Apostolate, headed by Detroit's Archbishop John F. Dearden (1907–1988), issued a statement printed in most diocesan newspapers.

> The introduction of the common language into the liturgical rites is an event of numerous and important implications. Clearly, it was the intention of the Fathers of the Second Vatican Council to provide people with rites of sacred worship which would be meaningful and intelligible to them. Both those parts of the liturgy which instruct the faithful, and those parts which express their prayer and devotion, are to be spoken or sung in the vernacular language. This reform in our custom is intended to bring the people into more effective contact with the sacred Scripture and the holy texts of the liturgy, thereby fostering deeper faith, greater knowledge, and more sincere prayer. But these worthy objectives will not automatically be achieved by the use of the vernacular. Such prayer and readings will have to be done in a more meaningful and appropriate manner than has unfortunately been employed by some priests when reciting Latin texts. To celebrate the liturgy in a manner that is apparently hasty, matter-of-fact, and without attention to the meaning of the words would, of course, be irreverent and improper no matter what language....[10]

Less than twelve months! That's the amount of preparation time the American Catholic Church had to implement the reformed liturgy. In retrospect, the transition to the vernacular was nothing short of miraculous. In this brief period, the United States bishops had to oversee and approve a new English translation and train a somewhat reluctant clergy in a new manner of conducting the liturgy. The latter was not an easy task, considering the ingrained habits many priests had with their beloved Latin Mass. They suddenly had to speak all the Mass prayers aloud, in a clear tone, not just at the sermon. Latin prayers committed to memory were exchanged for unfamiliar English texts that proved to be a stumbling block for many. Rubrics were also altered. Familiar gestures were gone, such as the Epistle being read on the on the right side of the altar and Gospel on the left, both recited softly in Latin while facing the sanctuary wall.[11]

Altar boys were retrained and lay readers recruited. Parish sound systems, usually consisting of a single microphone attached to the pulpit, were modified so the priest could be heard throughout the entire Mass, a real challenge in those pre-wireless days. Most importantly, the Catholic people needed education. The Mass had been a comfortable and reliable habit of quiet introspection for hundreds of years. Catholics now had to look up from their missals, put down their rosaries, and have an ongoing dialogue with their priest. In more progressive parishes, the congregation was even asked to sing! Catholics singing? Unthinkable! That faraway Council in Rome was now coming home to the people in the pews!

The liturgical education of American Catholics varied in quality from diocese to diocese, ranging anywhere between months-in-advance instructional homilies to a last-minute announcement the Sunday before the changeover. Thoughtful bishops allowed some parishes to experiment with English well before November 29, 1964. Many local liturgy commissions sponsored regional workshops and, perhaps taking a cue from Fitzpatrick, arranged for televised demonstration English Masses. The syndicated Catholic writers of the day were recruited to help explain the upcoming liturgical changes in their widely read columns. Mary Perkins Ryan wrote:

> The church is changing — not as to essentials, but in thinking out afresh and realizing in daily life what the essentials really mean. But this is something to be happy about, not afraid of. For many reasons, the Church has seemed unchanging in the last centuries, but this is not her normal state. She has to change to remain herself.... And we have to change if we are to be truly alive as Christians. Changelessness is not a property of living things. And so it is certainly good news, not bad, that we belong to a living Church.[12]

Equally important was the role of the liturgical publishers. What would the people hold in their hands to follow the new Mass? Cherished missals that were personal heirlooms would soon become obsolete. The transitional nature of the new translation was problematic. Something needed to be ready by the end of November, but the translations were still in process and might not even be ready in time to meet printing deadlines.

The Friends of the English Liturgy (FEL) published handy leaflets containing the English translation of the Mass, with a supplement of musical settings of the Mass Propers.[13]

Roger Nachtwey remembered: "Parishes could buy these inexpensively, five for a penny or something like that. We were sending thousands and thousands of them all over the country so the churches could distribute them in the pews on that First Sunday of Advent. It was simple: just one sheet of paper folded three times, with imprimatur [ecclesial approval]."[14]

Because of the already published *Demonstration English Mass*, FEL had an impressive head start in the race to get resources in the pews in time for the November 29, 1964, start of the new English Mass. However, their *English Liturgy Hymnal* would not be released until 1965. This gap provided another publisher an opportunity to step up to the plate and hit a homerun with a resource that would soon become the most popular Catholic hymnal in America.

·■·

Omer Westendorf (1916–1997) was born in Cincinnati, the youngest child of a very large German-American family. His mother supported her brood by operating a grocery store in the front parlor of their house. Westendorf received a degree in organ from Cincinnati's College of Music, followed by a Master's degree in Gregorian chant. He became choir director and organist at his home parish, Saint Bonaventure.

While serving in the infantry as a machine gunner during the Second World War, Westendorf was exposed to wonderful music from the choir lofts of Holland and Germany, with contemporary harmonies strikingly different from those of his own choir back home. He wanted to bring this music to America and he struck up a relationship with several European publishers who invited Omer to distribute their music in the United States. This was the 1950 birth of World Library of Sacred Music (WLSM), a name born of the company's original scope as a music importer. Westendorf had the foresight to pair English texts with these European melodies and World Library eventually became a publishing house.

In 1955, WLSM published the *The People's Hymnal,* a modest collection of hymns edited by Westendorf with the assistance of some seminarians from the Theological College at The Catholic University in Washington, DC. This landmark work contained traditional Protestant hymns, reworked European hymns, and new hymn texts by such future giants as Melvin Farrell (1930–1986), Michael Gannon (b. 1927), and Martin B. Hellriegel. The guiding principle behind the work was "that Christ's people may have the encouragement and means with which to take a more active and fruitful part in the Mass." Contrary to the syrupy sentimentality so prevalent in then-current devotional English hymnody, Westendorf took great care to ensure that his hymnals followed sound theological and liturgical praxis.

Westendorf's 1961 second edition of the *The People's Hymnal* put him well ahead of every other Catholic publisher in America at the time of the 1964 change to English. The now-titled *People's Mass Book* was the only hard-cover vernacular hymnal available to the parishes. Indeed, when samples were distributed during the St. Liturgical Week conference in August, almost every diocese placed orders, necessitating an unprecedented print run that saw eventual sales of more than two million copies over three years. With its distinctive stick-people logo, the *People's Mass Book* was an unqualified success.[15] Future editions would eventually incorporate Folk Mass songs by composers recruited by World Library. The most notable among this group of contemporary composers was the legendary Father Clarence Rivers (1931–2004).

Born into a Baptist family, young Clarence attended Catholic school in Cincinnati, where he grew to love the Church, especially its liturgy and traditions. His parents consented when he asked to be baptized. In 1956 Rivers became the first African American priest ordained for the Archdiocese of Cincinnati.

That alone was a major breakthrough in an American society (and Church) that was still racially segregated, but Father Rivers had more gifts to share, most notably his love of music. As a young priest, he dared to dream of the possibility that Catholics could worship in a style indigenous to the United States: the African American spiritual. Assigned as assistant pastor to Saint Joseph Church in the West End of Cincinnati, Rivers was encouraged by his pastor, Franciscan Father Clement J. Busemeyer, a progressive priest who welcomed liturgical experimentation. For example, at the liturgy of the pastor's silver jubilee in the priesthood, the children of his school sang *Missa Luba*, the famous African setting of the Latin Mass texts, notable for its Afrocentric percussion and tantalizing polyrhythmic vocals.

Inspired by his pastor's openness, Rivers began composing original English songs that empowered congregations of all cultures to embrace a more soulful way of singing. The Saint Joseph parishioners loved to sing their young priest's uplifting songs, and word of their lively liturgies spread far and wide. Providentially, neither Rivers nor his pastor ran into trouble with the Chancery for their innovations, done months before the promulgation of the Council's *Constitution on the Sacred Liturgy*.

Omer Westendorf heard about the excitement at Saint Joseph Parish and insisted on recording and publishing Rivers' music. *An American Mass Program* was released as an LP record in 1963. Radical yet unpretentious, this recording featured only the composer and a parish assembly singing his songs *a cappella* — no organ, no guitars, no piano.[16]

How groundbreaking was Father Rivers? Shortly after the release of *An American Mass Program,* he enrolled at The Catholic University of America in Washington, DC, to study drama. He ended up rubbing shoulders with prominent liturgists.

> Had I not been in Washington I could never have come into contact with the official and unofficial leadership of the Liturgical Conference, nor would I have been privileged to sit on its board; and I might never have been invited to share my "new" music with the American Church at the meeting of the Liturgical Conference in St. Louis at Kiel Auditorium in August of 1964. The Conference convened some 20,000 strong for the first Mass in English.[17]

That liturgy was a watershed for the liturgical movement. The prospect of participating in the first official English Mass in America attracted the largest crowd in the history of the Liturgical Conference. C. Alexander Peloquin (1918–1997), noted organist and liturgical composer, directed a choir that debuted his new classical-contemporary Mass setting. Sulpician Father Eugene Walsh (1911–1989), professor of liturgy at St. Mary's Seminary in Baltimore and already a recognized leader in the liturgical movement, directed the assembly in "full-throated song."[18] Dennis Fitzpatrick's setting of the Lord's Prayer from *Demonstration English Mass* was selected for this liturgy, an acknowledgment of his contributions to the movement. St. Louis seminarian Ray Repp attended as an eager participant.

> My interest at the time was the ecumenical possibilities of the new liturgy. And for me one of the high points of this service was the entire congregation singing "A Mighty Fortress" by Martin Luther. Putting all these elements together was, without a doubt, the real turning point of liturgical celebrations in America.[19]

The first official English Mass was the realization of a dream for the multitude of dedicated liturgists and reformers who had worked so hard to see that day. It was clearly the "full, conscious, and active participation" that the Council called for, and each new song roused the enthusiastic congregation into ever-increasing elation. Only something truly remarkable could top the already remarkable song list. Electricity filled the air when Clarence Rivers stepped up to the microphone at Communion to sing what would become his signature song. "God is love, and he who abides in love abides in God and God in him…."[20]

Blues notes! The "call and response" spiritual song structure! Scriptural lyrics expressed in idiomatic English! Passion in vocal interpretation! This was largely unheard of in the Roman liturgy. Rawn Harbor (b. 1947), coordinator of liturgy at the Franciscan School of Theology in Berkeley, California, said the song "had the assembly standing and applauding for 10 minutes."[21]

The American Catholic Church would never be the same after that first English Mass. The 20,000 conference participants departed from St. Louis enthralled and eager to bring that innovative spirit home.

・■・

There was a tangible feeling of excitement on that memorable First Sunday of Advent. Parishioners who were prepared by their priests ahead of time went to Church with great anticipation. Then there were those who were taken by complete surprise, wondering if they had accidentally wandered into a Protestant church. A new era had begun.

The *Catholic Sentinel* in Portland, Oregon, took a survey of parishioners as they departed their churches after that first English Mass. Their responses were generally positive.

"Frankly, for me, it's going to take some getting used to. I don't think it takes anything away from the Mass. And rather than be a stick-in-the-mud, I'll say I'm for it. I'm for progress."

"It will take me a while to get used to it. But the young people will get used to it quickly. I'm sure we will feel more like we're part of the Mass."

"We've worked up to this in our parish, so it didn't come as a shock, as it might have to some others. I think it's much more interesting. I'm a convert and it compares a great deal to the Protestant service. I think it's more understandable."

"I was pleasantly surprised. It would be helpful if the priest would speak up clearly, because in our parish it was sometimes difficult to follow him."

"I think it's going to take a while to get used to. You've been taught something all your life, and then all of a sudden it's changed. But I think it will be fine after things get to running as smoothly as they were before."

"I'm an older person and there are prayers I've said for years, and now I can't say them and follow the Mass. I can't see too well to read the missal, but it sounded good to me in English. I'm sure we'll get used to it."[22]

In the Diocese of Oakland, California, "a poll in October (1964) revealed that an overwhelming number of parishioners approved the change from Latin to English, though some lamented the loss of Latin. 'The Mass in Latin gave the feeling of home no matter where in the world you were attending.' Nonetheless, another poll in April 1967 revealed that people 'by and large' were in favor of the new liturgy. Another poll in 1972 indicated that more than 60% of the people polled felt the Mass had become more meaningful in the last five years."[23]

1964 is often remembered as the year of breathtaking change. In February, the Beatles changed popular music forever with an optimistic rock beat that roused American youth from the post-assassination blues. As the year unfolded, Congress passed the landmark Civil Rights Act, and Martin Luther King, Jr., was awarded the Nobel Peace Prize for his nonviolent resistance to racial oppression. By year's end, the American Catholic Church was also transformed. Within the context of such a dynamic social and political climate, the new English Mass was truly in step with the times.

---

1. Prendergast, Michael, and Ridge, M.D. editors, *Voices from the Council* (Portland, OR: Pastoral Press, 2004) 206.
2. "Those bishops who reacted at all (about 10%) were quite favorably impressed." From Devine, George, *Liturgical Renewal: An Agonizing Reappraisal* (Staten Island, NY: Alba House, 1973) 108. "Perhaps the voting of the bishops may have been influenced, at least to a degree, by this work of Fitzpatrick, for it is one possible solution of a timely and complex problem," From Hayburn, Fr. Robert F., "Mass in English Published in U.S.," *The Monitor*, November 29, 1963.
3. "Mass in English Up to U.S. Bishops" by George Weller, *Chicago Daily News*, November 14, 1963.
4. Rynne, Xavier, *Vatican Council II* (Maryknoll, New York: Farrar, Orbis Books, 1999) 72.
5. Ibid., 72.
6. Ibid., 73.
7. "*Sacrosanctum concilium* consists of 130 articles subdivided into seven chapters and an introduction. A declaration on revision of the calendar is appended to the text. Chapter one concerns general principles for the restoration and promotion of the liturgy and general norms for reform and renewal following upon these. Its 42 articles form the basis for a genuine renewal affecting theology and ecclesiology as well as sacrament and rite. Subsequent chapters, in sequence, address the Eucharist, other sacraments and sacramentals, the divine office, the liturgical year, sacred music, sacred art, and sacred furnishings." This summary from Winter, Miriam Therese, *Why Sing? Toward a Theology of Catholic Church Music* (Washington, DC: Pastoral Press, 1984) 47.

8 The Singing Nun, aka Sister Luc Gabriel, aka Jeanne-Paule Marie Deckers, was a nun of the Dominican order from Belgium. After captivating the world with her 1963 hit single about Saint Dominic, she caused a sensation with her January 5, 1964, television appearance on *The Ed Sullivan Show*. Broadcast via satellite hookup from her Fichermont convent, it was a rare public glimpse of the private world of cloistered nuns — another sign that the Catholic Church was opening up with the times.

9 "We used perhaps 20 translations that were already in existence," says the Rev. Frederick McManus (1923–2005), the new president of the Liturgical Conference. "It's purely experimental and provisional. The whole thing has to be done over." Most criticisms stressed the Mass's "rough spots." Bishop Charles Buswell (1913–2008) of Pueblo, Colorado, suggested that "we need to get the you-who out of the Gloria," meaning the part that now goes "You, who take away the sins of the world, have mercy on us." From *Time* magazine, September 4, 1964.

10 *The Use of the Vernacular at Mass*, Statement, Bishops' Commission on the Liturgical Apostolate, November 1964, from McManus, Frederick R., *Thirty Years of Liturgical Renewal: Statements of the Bishops' Committee on the Liturgy* (Washington, DC: United States Catholic Conference, 1987) 26–29. This statement also contained many practical suggestions for praying and speaking aloud.

11 Msgr. Frederick R. McManus, first executive secretary for the Secretariat of the US Bishops' Committee on the Liturgy (BCL), had this observation: "In 1964, and, indeed, in each successive expansion of permitted vernacular in the Mass, the individual diocesan bishop was faced with a pastoral question. While the Catholic people might be favorable to the liturgical vernacular (later surveys showed this to be an overwhelming preference of the people), many priests exercising the pastoral office were not prepared for and not desirous of the change. The vernacular was unsettling to priests who were in a tradition of silent Masses, hurried Masses, routine Masses. In many dioceses, therefore, the date for the initial concession of the vernacular became also, by episcopal decree, the date for a required use of the vernacular in regularly scheduled Masses with congregations of the people…. From a pastoral viewpoint, it is certain that a mere permission to use the vernacular in a given diocese would have resulted in the most diverse practices — and, in the days before parish councils and worship committees, would have deprived a very large percentage of the Catholic people of the fruits of the Council's first decision." From McManus, Frederick R., *Thirty Years of Liturgical Renewal: Statements of the Bishops' Committee on the Liturgy* (Washington, DC: United States Catholic Conference, 1987) 106–107.

12 Ryan, Mary Perkins, *Has the New Liturgy Changed You*? (a collection of the author's syndicated newspaper columns) (New York: Paulist Press, 1967) 4.

13 The Mass Propers are the changeable texts of the liturgy that are particular to a given feast or liturgical date, e.g., Christmas or Easter Sunday. These changeable texts include the prayers of the assembly (the entrance antiphon, the response after the first reading, the Communion song, etc.) and the prayers of the priest (collect/opening prayer, secret/prayer over the gifts, etc.). This is in contrast with the unchangeable texts known as Mass Ordinaries (now called Mass settings): *Kyrie*/Lord, Have Mercy, *Gloria*/Glory to God, *Sanctus*/Holy, etc.

14 Interview with the author, March 6, 2004, Portland, Oregon, by phone to Shawano, Wisconsin.

15 Sources: *The Cincinnati Post*, obituary of October 23, 1997; World Library Publications in-house biography of Omer Westendorf.

16 For a fuller treatment of Father Rivers, see "Freeing the Spirit: Very Personal Reflections on One Man's Search for the Spirit in Worship," an autobiographical article by Clarence-Rufus J. Rivers, PhD., that appeared in *US Catholic Historian,* Spring 2001, Volume 19, Number 2, 95–143.

17 Ibid.

18 Leonard, Timothy, *Geno: A Biography of Eugene Walsh, SS* (Washington, DC: Pastoral Press, 1988) 83.

19 Interview with the author, April 11, 2008.

20 "God Is Love" by Clarence Rivers, © 1964, 1968, World Library Publications.

21 *National Catholic Reporter*, "Fr. Clarence Rivers, liturgy pioneer, dead at 73," January 7, 2005.

22 *Catholic Sentinel* (Archdiocese of Portland in Oregon), Volume 95, Number 49. December 4, 1964.

23 Burns, Jeffrey M., and Batiza, Mary Carmen, *We Are the Church: A History of the Diocese of Oakland* (Strasbourg, France: Editions du Signe, 2001) 50.

Chapter Five
"Keep the Fire Burning"

> Thousands of Americans answered Kennedy and [Thomas] Merton's call, basing their commitment on the traditions of their Judeo-Christian faith. Theirs was not just a struggle against poverty, but a repudiation of the twin towers of consumerism and conformity, two forces that took hold of the nation in the 1950s and refused to let go. Theirs was a growing awareness that there was more to life than a two-car garage and a new Frigidaire.[1]
>
> —Don Lattin, religion reporter, *San Francisco Chronicle*

"Father, may I lead some music at our Mass?" Ray Repp asked. He was one of 400 college-age volunteers attending the orientation in Chicago of the Catholic Church Extension Society's Lay Volunteer Program, which sent young people to work with the poor throughout America. The program included a late-afternoon Mass, and the first day's liturgy was celebrated with no music. It was the summer of 1965 and American Catholics were just getting accustomed to the new English Mass.

"Of course," the priest replied. "Do you play the organ?" "Well, all I have is my guitar, plus a few songs I've written." Repp knew it was a shot in the dark and the priest would probably decline his offer. The priest's response was a pleasant surprise. "Let's try it!"[2]

Imagine the excitement of the next day's liturgy in a chapel filled with recent college graduates from around the country. Newly arrived, their youthful idealism and enthusiasm quickly bonded them, together with their common goal of going out into the world to serve Christ's poor.

The young composer greeted the eager congregation, his Gibson guitar slung over his left shoulder. "Good evening. Tonight for Mass we're going to sing some new songs. The first one goes like this." He launched into a song that would soon become an anthem for young Catholics everywhere:

> Here we are, all together as we sing our song joyfully.
> Here we are, joined together as we pray we'll always be.
>
> Join we now as friends and celebrate the brotherhood we share all as one.
> Keep the fire burning, kindle it with care, and we'll all join in and sing!
> © 1966, Otter Creek Music. Published by OCP. All rights reserved.

The youthful congregation was electrified. This new music was as fresh as anything sung by Peter, Paul & Mary, and they chimed in readily when Repp invited them to sing along.

And so the Mass began, as the chapel began to rock with a sound previously unheard in the Roman liturgy. As the priest processed to the altar, every one of those 400 Extension volunteers sang "Here We Are" at the top of their lungs. They continued at the offertory with "Of My Hands," followed by Repp's haunting "Hear, O Lord" at Communion. By the time they sang "Forevermore" at the conclusion of Mass, there was a palpable sense of breakthrough. The young students couldn't help but to break into applause after Repp's final strum.

Repp himself was taken aback by the enthusiastic response to his songs. When he composed at the seminary he was experimenting with song forms, trying to imagine how the ancient psalms might be interpreted in a modern folk idiom. There was never any intention of performing these songs at Mass, much less of starting a liturgical revolution. Because the young adults celebrated liturgy daily, Repp needed to quickly compose new songs to keep the repertoire fresh. From these ad hoc sessions emerged the beginnings of the *Mass for Young Americans*.[3]

"During our month-long orientation in Chicago we had classes in psychology, sociology, and other areas that would be useful for our work," Repp recalled. "We also took daily field trips to work with the poor in the inner city of Chicago. I had never witnessed such poverty before this time. The Chicago Department of Social Services taught us a great deal about how to put people in touch with resources to help themselves. My new songs were inspired by the experiences I was having while visiting the people in the inner city during the day."[4]

By the end of their month together, the Extension volunteers had become very close. In addition to singing at Mass, they often stayed up late at night singing together on the lawn. Repp had become a master of the folk repertoire and the group loved singing anything he performed. As the time drew near for departure to their assigned communities, Repp's friends urged him to collect his music in a booklet as a souvenir of their time together. Ray spent a few late nights printing his song booklet in the ubiquitous purple ditto medium[5] that would ironically prove to be the undoing of his future publisher.

On the final day of the orientation program, Repp's friends were pleased to receive his gift of the songs that had come to mean so much to them. Amidst tearful and emotional goodbyes, this remarkable group of young adults was sent out to every one of the 48 continental states. Assigned to work in Salt Lake City, Repp smiled thoughtfully as his plane landed in the community that would be his home for a year. The Chicago orientation had been a marvelous experience, and the young composer felt validated by the enthusiastic acceptance of his music. He also thought it was a unique one-time circumstance and gave no more thought to ever performing those songs at liturgy again.

"I was working in connection with the cathedral [of the Madeleine in Salt Lake City] in addition to working with the poor and the derelicts, and all sorts of other things I was doing," Repp recalled. "And because they noticed that I could sing, they asked me to be the cantor. I was leading music in the cathedral every week. It was 'Holy God, We Praise Thy Name,' and all that other kind of stuff. And I wasn't using my guitar, I assure you."[6]

Repp had developed a growing commitment to social justice issues. Earlier in the year he left his seminary without permission, hopping on a bus bound for Alabama, to join in Martin Luther King, Jr.'s march from Selma to Montgomery.

"This was the beginning of a major change inside my head," Repp remembers. "After witnessing some of the brutality on the part of the police and hearing Dr. King speak, I knew I had to become part of the solution instead of part of the problem. The songs I began writing became even more focused on the Gospel's call to 'live together in peace.'"[7]

In this regard, young Ray was following in a tradition established by Benedictine Father Virgil Michel and his attempts in the 1930s to bring the European efforts in liturgical reform to the United States. According to Michel, lay people needed to be educated in the liturgy and empowered to participate. This meant, among other things, Dialogue Masses, congregational singing of Gregorian chant, and lay recitation of the Divine Office, truly radical ideas in the 1930s and 40s. The time was right for such thinking, and Michel soon found ready followers who were willing to take up the torch for liturgical renewal.

Fr. Michel had an enormously full schedule of teaching at seminaries, speaking at conferences, writing for *Orate Fratres*[8] magazine, and establishing the Liturgical Press, an eventual giant in Catholic publishing. By 1930, Michel was exhausted and in April of that year suffered a nervous breakdown. Ordered to rest by his superiors, Michel spent two months in the hospital, then further recuperated at the Chippewa Indian Reservation in northern Minnesota in beautiful natural surroundings. As he recovered, Michel eventually became involved in pastoral ministry with his Native American hosts.

Michel's time with the Chippewa was invigorating and transformative. He learned their language, hunted and fished, ate, worked and relaxed with them, and sought them out to invite them to Mass. Although continuing to suffer insomnia, headaches, and depression, Michel's ministry at the reservation gave him a greater awareness of the many injustices that were an everyday part of Native American life. When he returned to his work in liturgical reform, Virgil Michel was a changed man.[9]

Grounding himself in the official teachings of the Church, Michel used papal teaching as his basic thesis or syllogism on the link between liturgy and social justice. In a 1934 article in *Orate Fratres* entitled "Liturgy: The Basis of Social Regeneration," Michel put together the ideas of two popes:

> Pius X tells us that the liturgy is the indispensable source of the true Christian spirit; Pius XI says that the true Christian spirit is indispensable for social regeneration. Hence, the conclusion: The liturgy is the indispensable basis for social regeneration.[10]

Practicing what he preached, Michel befriended Dorothy Day (1897–1980) and Peter Maurin (1877–1949) of the Catholic Worker movement (established in 1933). He encouraged them to ground their work in the daily celebration of the Eucharist. Already well-versed in Benedictine spirituality, Day welcomed Michel's insights and saw in the liturgy the means by which society could be transformed. Michel also worked with (now Servant of God) Baroness Catherine De Hueck, founder of Friendship House (established in the early 1930s), a social justice movement that floundered until Michel spoke with them.

> How fortunate you are.... This is what I have been dreaming about. You are discouraged. You need the Mass. You must persevere by all means. Study the Mass, live the Mass. Between two Masses you can bear anything.[11]

De Hueck was moved by Michel's encouragement and began to see immediate results. She wrote:

> In the liturgy we learn to know Christ. And if we truly know him, we shall recognize him everywhere, but especially in his poor....[12]

Michel's efforts were validated in part by Pope Pius XII's landmark 1943 encyclical, *Mystici Corporis Christi* (*Church as the Mystical Body of Christ*), which presented Saint Paul's image of Christ's Mystical Body as a central model of the Church. Already a hot topic of discussion among theologians throughout the first half of the twentieth century, the publication of this encyclical was seen by progressives as a papal endorsement of their understanding that the Church was a united whole of many parts — pope, bishops, priests, *and* lay people. In this view, Christians were united as the Mystical Body with Christ as its head. Members of this Body could not be thought of as mere individuals but as a corporate whole that would have concern for all. The Eucharist was seen as the perfect sign of this unity. This thinking empowered the liturgical movement, and Msgr. Reynold Hillenbrand spoke passionately on the topic.

> The Mystical Body provides the compelling reason, the driving force to set things right. The Body is one, a living Whole. What one group suffers, all suffer — whether that be the politically enslaved in the South Seas, the economically exploited in Bolivia, the starving in China, or the racially disenfranchised at home. We must see Christ in all his members, and at the same time remember that all men are destined to be his members. We must have a deep, intimate, living conviction of it. And we will acquire that conviction at Mass, where we are one at Sacrifice![13]

The author of the encyclical put it even more bluntly:

> "How can we claim to love the Divine Redeemer, if we hate those whom he has redeemed with his precious blood, so that he might make them members of his Mystical Body? ...[I]t should be said that the more we become 'members of one another,' 'mutually careful one for another,' the closer we shall be united with God and with Christ...."[14]

Pius XII's subsequent interactions with the liturgy seem, in hindsight, to have supported the encyclical's progressive outlook and pointed the way to the further reforms of Vatican II. In 1955, Pius instigated the first official changes in the liturgy since the Council of Trent (1545–1563) when he revised the liturgy of Holy Week. He also encouraged modern critical study of the Bible, and wrote an encyclical that directly addressed the liturgy, *Mediator Dei* (1947), which was very influential for the Council's *Constitution on the Sacred Liturgy*.

Ironically, this connection between liturgy and social justice, so grounded in theology and in practicum, was not generally taught in seminaries, outside of Chicago's Mundelein Seminary where Msgr. Hillenbrand served as rector.

"We did study the social justice encyclicals[15] in the seminary," Ray Repp recalls. "However, I don't remember the social justice aspects emphasized. We had no course specifically on social justice. Remember, during most of my time in the sem, we were using Latin textbooks to study philosophy and theology. There were not a lot of social justice themes in those books."

Instead of relying on the teachings of Virgil Michel and other reformers, Repp and his fellow seminarians learned by doing. Swept up by the changing times and by President Kennedy's call to volunteerism, seminarians in the early 1960s joined marches and demonstrations and volunteered on their own, often without the approval of their superiors.

"My interest in social justice did not come from the seminary at all," said Repp. "If anything, it was a reaction to the seminary. I was fortunate at Kendrick Seminary (St. Louis) to be only a short distance from Webster College. At the time this private Catholic college was offering very progressive courses in theology, Scripture, and social justice. I found myself 'sneaking' out to sit in on some classes and getting involved in a lot of group discussions. These kind[s] of discussions didn't take place in our seminary."[16]

Of course, the secular folk music movement added more fuel as popular singers began addressing the injustices around them. Folk Mass composer Jack Miffleton, a seminarian at St. Mary's Seminary in Baltimore from 1960–1968, has this recollection:

"There was a folk music revival on college campuses. Soon, many of us were strumming guitars and learning both old folk songs and songs by Joan Baez, Bob Dylan, Gordon Lightfoot, and Judy Collins. In 1963, we joined our voices with Baez and others in Martin Luther King, Jr.'s march in Washington. I became involved in the civil rights movement and later anti-war movements through this style of music."[17]

The Folk Mass composers' connection with the social justice movements of their seminary years is important. While the documents of Vatican II, unread by most Catholics, waxed eloquently on the need for social reform in *Gaudium et Spes* (1965) and other decrees, the Folk Mass composers put those themes into the hands of the people. Their appealing songs united congregations and helped them reflect on the issues *while they were at Eucharist.* Miffleton wrote "But Then Comes the Morning" which had the line "Look at him nailed to the cross, nailed by our lack of concern." Carey Landry sang optimistically that "The Spirit is a-movin' all over, all over this land." The Dameans would sing of "The New Creation" and the need to "hear the voice of the prophets living today." Repp himself composed the energizing "Till All My People Are One."

> Stand together for what you believe.
> Work for what must be done.
> Love each other in all that you do,
> Till all my people are one.
> © 1967, Otter Creek Music. Published by OCP. All rights reserved.

All of this was in the near future in the summer of 1965 when Ray Repp was focusing on serving the poor in Salt Lake City. He had no idea that his music that so enlivened the Extension orientation program was already causing a revolution of sorts around the country.

It was spontaneous and grassroots. There was no pre-meditated marketing plan, no clear strategy or conscious campaign. All Repp did was give his fellow students a cheaply printed copy of the folk songs that they sang at Mass for their memorable orientation session. It was a keepsake, a thoughtful gesture, and nothing more. What Repp actually did, innocently enough, was to send out 400 ambassadors of his music to the 48 continental states. Such was the power of Repp's early songs that no recording was necessary. The melodies were so catchy and the guitar chords so easy that, in the tradition of all true folk songs, person-to-person transmission was all that was necessary. That, and the ever-accessible purple ditto machine.

And so, Repp's friends sang his songs from the inner cities of Chicago, New York, and San Francisco, to the rural Appalachians and Deep South. "Here We Are," "Come Away," and "Forevermore" were sung at liturgies throughout America, to great acclaim. Suddenly, the Mass was entirely new yet again. Word got out and people started flocking to these "Folk Masses," charmed by their spontaneity and spirit. Copies of the lyrics were happily distributed to newcomers who requested them and, in the grand folk music tradition of oral transmission, Repp's songs grew in popularity and demand.

Ironically, this burst of Folk Mass enthusiasm happened everywhere except in the relatively isolated confines of Salt Lake City, where Repp continued to sing Gregorian chant and lead traditional hymns at the Cathedral of the Madeleine. The young composer had no idea of the revolution he helped to create. Several weeks later, Repp was surprised and startled to receive a phone call from Chicago. It was Dennis Fitzpatrick from Friends of the English Liturgy (FEL).

"We would like to make a record of your music."

---

1. Lattin, Don, *Following Our Bliss: How the Spiritual Ideals of the Sixties Shape Our Lives Today* (San Francisco: HarperSanFrancisco, 2003) 31.
2. The priest, Monsignor John May (1922–1994), would become the archbishop of St. Louis in 1980.
3. Fr. (now Monsignor) Joe James (b. 1932), a priest of the Diocese of Amarillo, Texas, was assisting at the Extension orientation. "I had a trusty little reel-to-reel tape recorder that I used to carry around so I could record anything of note," said Fr. James. "This guy [Repp] was singing some songs that I thought were really great. So I recorded them." As will be seen in the next chapter, this informal recording would prove to be a catalyst for the Folk Mass movement. (See "Texas priest seen as 'godfather' of nascent liturgical movement" by Jessica Kelly, Catholic News Service, December 14, 2007.)
4. Interview for an Internet article.
5. In the days before laser printers and photocopiers, schools and churches printed multiple copies of bulletins, class notes, and songbooks via a primitive medium called ditto. The writer simply typed or handwrote text on a two-ply master sheet. The second sheet was coated with a layer of colored wax, and the pressure of typing or writing on the top sheet transferred the colored wax to its backside, creating a stencil for printing. The completed top sheet was attached to a drum on a "spirit duplicator" or ditto machine through which paper was fed by a hand crank. A sweet-smelling alcohol caused the stencil to print out in the color purple, and many school children of this era remember bringing freshly dittoed copies to their noses as teachers distributed them in their classroom. Mimeograph was an alternate reproduction technique that utilized black ink. These inexpensive printing systems were a big factor in the speedy (and illegal) distribution of the early Folk Mass music.
6. Interview by author, October 1, 2004, Portland, Oregon, by phone to Ferrisburg, Vermont.
7. Interview for an Internet article.
8. Later known as *Worship*.
9. For a fuller treatment on the life and work of Virgil Michel, see Pecklers, Keith, *The Unread Vision: The Liturgical Movement in the United States of America: 1926–1955* (Collegeville: Liturgical Press, 1998).
10. Michel, OSB, Virgil, "Liturgy: The Basis of Social Regeneration," *Orate Fratres*, Volume 9 (Collegeville, MN: Liturgical Press, 1934–35) 545.
11. Interview with Catherine De Hueck, Washington, DC, February 5, 1953. Quoted in Marx, 379. As quoted in Pecklers, Keith, *The Unread Vision: The Liturgical Movement in the United States of America: 1926–1955* (Collegeville: Liturgical Press, 1998) 116.
12. De Hueck, "I Saw Christ Today," 310. As quoted in Pecklers, Keith, *The Unread Vision: The Liturgical Movement in the United States of America: 1926–1955* (Collegeville: Liturgical Press, 1998) 116.
13. Hillenbrand, Reynold, "The Spirit of Sacrifice in Christian Society: Statement of Principle," in *National Liturgical Week 1943* (Ferdinand, IN.: The Liturgical Conference, 1944), 106. As quoted in Pecklers, Keith, *The Unread Vision: The Liturgical Movement in the United States of America: 1926–1955* (Collegeville: Liturgical Press, 1998) 147.
14. Pope Pius XII, *Mystici Corporis Christi* (1943) paragraph 74.
15. The great social justice encyclicals included Leo XIII's *Rerum Novarum* (1891), Pius XI's *Quadragesimo Anno* (1931) and, of course, Pius XII's *Mystici Corporis Christi*.
16. Interview by author, October 1, 2004, Portland, Oregon, by phone to Ferrisburg, Vermont.
17. Interview with the author, November 15, 2004, from Martinez, California

Chapter Six
Mass for Young Americans

Campbell: Even in the Roman Catholic Church, my God — they've translated the Mass out of the ritual language and into a language that has a lot of domestic associations. The Latin of the Mass was a language that threw you out of the field of domesticity. The altar was turned so that the priest's back was to you, and with him you addressed yourself outward. Now they've turned the altar around — it looks like Julia Child giving a demonstration — all homey and comfy.
Moyers: And they play a guitar.
Campbell: They play a guitar. They've forgotten that the function of ritual is to pitch you out, not to wrap you in where you have been all the time.[1]

—from *The Power of Myth*

By the mid-1960s, Dennis Fitzpatrick could be justifiably proud of the accomplishments of his young life. He had developed a viable and critically acclaimed system of English chant. His *Demonstration English Mass* attracted standing-room-only crowds, garnered laudatory reviews from around the country, and was influential as an English prototype for the Council Fathers at Vatican II. When the Mass officially changed to English, Fitzpatrick was ready, offering inexpensive transitional leaflets with the new English texts that grateful parishes around the country snapped up in droves.

In early 1965, Fitzpatrick knew he had an opportunity to supply his transitional Mass leaflet customers with a more permanent resource. Thus was born the *English Liturgy Hymnal,* a thick, comprehensive hard-bound volume that presumed a celebration of the new liturgy in the spirit of the *Demonstration English Mass.* Unlike World Library's *People's Mass Book,* which mentioned the Mass Propers only in a brief parenthetical summary, the *English Liturgy Hymnal* featured page after page of English refrains for the Mass Propers, supplemented with verses meticulously marked for the Fitzpatrick psalmody.

In retrospect, this emphasis on the officially prescribed Mass text was both correct and ahead of its time.[2] But World Library's preference for hymn substitution — in place of the Mass Propers — won the popularity battle and ultimately led to the unfortunate "four hymn" pattern of congregational singing that characterized American Catholic worship for many years, with music sung only at the entrance, the offertory, the Communion, and at the recessional.

The *English Liturgy Hymnal* did have a hymn section, but it was buried between the Propers and Fitzpatrick psalmody. Indeed, FEL's hymnal didn't even give titles for the hymns, designating them only by their metrical markings,[3] with a small-print title for reference only. Meanwhile, congregations singing from the World Library hymnal grew to love and identify with such clearly titled hymn favorites as "Sing Praise to Our Creator," "Where Charity and Love Prevail," and "God Is Love."

Fitzpatrick gambled that his emphasis on chanted Mass Propers and English psalmody would win broad acceptance. It was not meant to be. *People's Mass Book* became a best seller. *English Liturgy Hymnal* sold modestly and was not the commercial windfall that Fitzpatrick anticipated. The promulgation of the vernacular liturgy made the *Demonstration English Mass* unnecessary. Friends of the English Liturgy was being pressured to both meet its bills and pay its investors. Clearly, FEL needed to find another niche in the liturgical market to give them an edge over their competitors.

Fitzpatrick and Nachtwey continued to lead their music at liturgical conferences and similar events throughout the Midwest to promote the *English Liturgy Hymnal*. In 1965, at Creighton University in Omaha, the National Council of Christians and Jews held one such conference, organized by their friend, Monsignor Daniel Cantwell (1915–1996) of Chicago. A disciple of Monsignor Hillenbrand, Cantwell was renowned as a leader in social justice ministry, serving as chaplain for such lay organizations as the Labor Alliance, Friendship House, and the Catholic Interracial Council. Nachtwey remembered the Omaha conference wistfully.

"Monsignor [Cantwell] sent an SOS to Dennis, saying 'We're planning the daily conference liturgies and now I have a bunch of students out here carrying guitars and demanding to sing for the liturgy!' Dennis and I had done many liturgies for Dan Cantwell's events, utilizing our English chant, and this is what Monsignor was expecting for this conference. And he was upset about the idea of these kids bringing guitars.

"He said to Dennis, 'Please come here and prepare the Masses for our convention this week. I want you to do it yourself so we know exactly what's going to happen.' Well, Dennis had something else going on and he replied, 'May I send Roger?' So I went to Omaha and took care of Dan's liturgies there.

"A week or two after I had 'saved' Monsignor from this 'horrible' guitar stuff, Dennis called me at our Chicago office one night from his home. Our staff and I had been working around the clock, getting the *English Liturgy Hymnal* out in time for the Liturgical Week that summer in Baltimore. And Dennis said, 'Could you please take an hour or so and come over here? I have something very serious to talk about.' And I thought, 'Oh, my God! What's going to happen now?' Because we went through one disaster after another in those days.

"So I arrived at his house and he had a drink for me. We sat down and he said, 'Okay, listen to this.' He punched on his tape recorder and it was a group of young people singing the songs of Ray Repp. After we listened, Dennis asked me, 'What do you think about this?' And I said, 'Well, that's what we saved Monsignor from, isn't it?'"[4]

Fitzpatrick picks up the narrative from here. "I received this recording in the mail of a Folk Mass by Ray Repp. And I remember listening to it and thinking, 'I don't care for this much.' I played it for Roger and he didn't care much for it, either. I didn't know anybody who cared much for it because it was such a different, novel idea. I didn't go for guitars. It wasn't classical music, what I liked. It had no connection with Gregorian chant.

"I wasn't interested in publishing other composers. I was interested in what I was doing, and when this liturgical thing was over I wanted to get back into composing contemporary classical music. And then Repp's music came in. But then I listened to it a second time, a third time. And what I began to like about it was his text, more than the music. And then I heard that some bishops were prohibiting the use of these kinds of texts. My texts were acceptable because they were scriptural translations. His texts were freely composed texts that were not necessarily Scripture-based.

"And then I heard that young people who wanted to worship with that kind of material were being forbidden to do it. When I heard that I really got annoyed. Although I did not like folk music, I also did not like anybody telling somebody else how they had to worship. I think that really irritated me more than anything else, and that probably motivated me to publish it, because nobody else would. They were afraid. The publishers were terrified of the bishops because they thought their sales would fall through the floor if they didn't get approval.

"Repp's music was catchy. I liked that part, but it wasn't what I call high art. It took a while for me to overcome that attitude. But what really did it for me was when I heard that these kids had their music taken away and told that they couldn't worship this way. That, on top of the Church trying to control me, and my ongoing irritation with the hierarchy for five years by that time — that was enough. I didn't care if it sold or not. I didn't care if it had financial consequences at all. That didn't bother me one bit. So I published it. To hell with the imprimatur."[5]

Ray Repp continues the story. "About a month after I started to work in Salt Lake City, I received a phone call from Dennis Fitzpatrick in Chicago. He called me. I didn't send him anything. Obviously, someone from Extension sent my music to Dennis,[6] and he called me and said, 'Would you come to Chicago and record an album?' And I thought, 'I don't know who this person is, but he's crazy!' And I said, 'Sure, I can do it.' And I went to St. Louis, actually, and recorded the album, then went back to what I was doing and didn't think about the record anymore."[7]

Fitzpatrick's decision to record and publish Repp's music proved to be revolutionary. Released in February 1966, *Mass for Young Americans* was simple and deliberately unpretentious. Although Repp was the featured artist, the real stars were his catchy Folk Mass songs.

"We recorded in one evening," Repp recalls. "And I called the rector at my seminary in St. Louis and said, 'I'm doing a recording. May I have permission to ask twenty of the guys to go beyond their Lights Out and come to the recording studio?' And it took a little talking, too, because the seminary was really strict in those days. But we received permission and went into the studio and, four or five hours later, we were finished recording the album. That was it. We did it like a concert. There was no production whatsoever."[8]

Listening to *Mass for Young Americans* today, one is struck by its stark sound. In fact, it was meant to be a demonstration recording, rather than a record for listening, similar in scope to its predecessor, *Demonstration English Mass*. In this format, musicians could get a sense for the feel and the tempos, allowing them to perform Repp's songs the same way at their own liturgies.

Everything about the album cover was certainly earnest and calculated to appeal to pastors and music directors taking their first cautious step into this new style for liturgy.

> The question of the use of folk-type music during the celebration of the liturgy has caused quite a furor. It is a question that is generally answered with extreme opinions. Folk-type music has been banned in some dioceses and found acceptance in others. Is folk-type music worthy of the house of God?
>
> The composer states his case in these words: "Just as we have many types of people with various backgrounds and tastes, so we should have various types of music through which these people can express themselves in a meaningful way. What is worthy of the People of God must surely be worthy of the house of God."[9]

The track listing was a veritable hymn board for American Catholics in 1966. Beginning with the title Mass setting, the album continued with "Sons of God" (by James Thiem, OSB), "Here We Are," "And I Will Follow (Psalm 23)," "Forevermore (Psalm 117)," "Clap Your Hands (Psalm 47)," "Hear, O Lord," "Come Away," "Of My Hands," "Shout from the Highest Mountain," and "I'm Not Afraid." These songs are burned into the collective subconscious of Baby Boomer Catholics who, for better or for worse, built their youthful liturgical memories around an informal and spirited Folk Mass that was 180 degrees removed from the quiet introspective liturgy of their parents and grandparents.

The response to *Mass for Young Americans* was immediate.

> I was rather pleased with the Mass by Mr. Repp, although I continue to protest that I have no musical appreciation in these matters. Perhaps I wasn't supposed to have the following reaction, but certain parts of it seemed to me extremely dignified and impressive and even traditional! And I was a little reminded of some of the Indian and other Mass chants that we heard at the Council.
> Father Frederick R. McManus
> Bishops' Commission on the Liturgical Apostolate
> March 16, 1966

Mr. Repp's Mass is one that I have tried out with success for young people and folk specialists. In their judgment it is both prayerful and easily doable.
Clement J. McNaspy, SJ
America magazine (Jesuit)
April 9, 1966

To say that Repp's *Mass for Young Americans* and the whole idea of the Mass sung in the folk idiom has caught on like wildfire is to do no more than state plain fact. The great appeal of his music rests partly on the idea of singing the old responses in a new way, of translating Christ's message into the idiom of the coffeehouse.[10]
Bruce Cook
U.S. Catholic magazine
May 1967

It is obvious that we and our generation do not completely understand our youngsters; most of us are quite satisfied with the religious services we were brought up in. It is to the credit of the churches — and particularly the Roman Catholic and Anglican (Episcopal) — that they are not smugly waiting for this under-30 generation to "come over"; they are experimenting and coming up with music and services that appeal to this age group. Mr. Repp's first disc is a consistent bestseller of its type.
Review from *The New Records: The Oldest Record Magazine in America*
H. Royer Smith Company
Vol. 35, No. 7, September 1967

Mr. Repp's music has been tremendously successful with all the groups with which I have used it.
Rev. Clarence J. Rivers, composer of *An American Mass Program*[11]

Was Ray Repp the first Folk Mass composer? An argument could be made that Clarence Rivers has claim to that title because the release of his *An American Mass Program* pre-dated *Mass for Young Americans* by two years and was undeniably influential. But Rivers' music was of a quality and sophistication that was more in line with such contemporary classical composers as Jan Vermulst (1925–1994), Flor Peters (1903–1986), and Spiritan Father Lucien Deiss (1921–2007). In keeping with the cautious yet groundbreaking outlook common in liturgy in 1963, Rivers' *An American Mass Program* was an almost chant-like production, featuring cantors and choir singing *a cappella*, albeit with the unique breakthrough of the vernacular language as expressed in the gospel feel of the African American spiritual.

In an age when the Black community was still struggling for recognition and acceptance, Rivers' music may have been challenging for many white Catholic musicians. They needed education to learn and appreciate the rhythms and nuances of the Black music experience. Father Rivers dedicated his life to teaching Catholics a more soulful (he said "soul-full") way of singing, through his concerts, workshops, articles, books, advocacy and, of course, his compelling songs. Rivers' music was critically acclaimed, but Catholic composers inspired by the commercial folk style of the early 1960s enjoyed more immediate popularity.

An argument could also be made that the young Jesuit Paul Quinlan (b. 1939) was the first Catholic folk artist. His *Glory Bound* album was released by the America Record Society in 1965 and distributed by World Library of Sacred Music. With the subtitle "Psalms Set to Folk Music," *Glory Bound* was a lively collection of folk songs that utilized the ancient poetry of the Old Testament as source material. According to the album's liner notes (co-written by noted folk musician Oscar Brand [b. 1920] and Catholic music critic Jesuit Father Clement J. McNaspy [1915–1995]), Quinlan, dubbed "the Jesuit Folksinger" on the cover, had been performing these songs "for a wide range of listeners — ministers, rabbis, priests, seminarians, as well as young and old lay folk of many faiths. Their enthusiasm, as well as my own and that of several of my colleagues, prompted the America Record Society to present this first recording of folk-psalms."[12]

Although these Quinlan songs surely were sung at experimental liturgies in 1965, it is interesting to note that none of these folk-psalms were part of the original national repertoire of Folk Mass songs, nor did they appear in 1967's *Hymnal for Young Christians*.[13] Quinlan did go on to record an album of liturgical music for FEL (1967's *Run Like a Deer*), and the composer found even greater acclaim with his later Folk Mass classic, "It's a Brand New Day." *Glory Bound* is probably best seen in context of the explosion of folk artists that permeated the secular record industry in the mid-1960s.[14]

Ray Repp was the first documented Roman Catholic composer to set the official Mass text to folk guitar music. His 1965 summer Extension volunteer experience is certainly a concrete starting point that gave grassroots exposure to such songs as "Here We Are," "Of My Hands," and "Hear, O Lord," all of which became instant national favorites even without radio exposure. Repp's early songs were lightning in a bottle, embodying the proletarian spirit of secular folk music at its best.[15]

Repp's primacy is cited by no less an authority than the *Encyclopedia of Contemporary Christian Music* by Mark Allan Powell (b. 1953). A thick comprehensive survey of the Protestant contemporary Christian music scene, this encyclopedia devotes a whole page to the Catholic composer.

> Ray Repp is the earliest of all the pioneers of contemporary Christian music. To quote *Jesus Music* magazine, he can be considered as "the guy who started it all." The history of contemporary Christian music usually traces the genre to the Jesus movement revival of the early '70s, which is when it emerged as a recognizable entity outside the church. Half a decade earlier, however, Repp and a handful of others (Ralph Carmichael [b. 1927], John Fischer [b. 1947],[16] Kurt Kaiser [b. 1934], and John

C. Ylvisaker [b. 1934]) were creating youth-oriented music within the church that would pave the way for acceptance of the secular-sounding Jesus music when the revival hit. Of these forerunners, Repp was easily the most significant within America's mainline denominations, especially those churches that had their historical origins in Europe (Roman Catholic, Episcopalian, Lutheran, Presbyterian, and some Methodists). It is unlikely that any single artist has ever had the monopoly of influence that he either enjoyed or endured for the four years spanning 1966-1969.[17]

Because of Ray Repp and the *Mass for Young Americans*, the name of FEL Publications became synonymous with the Folk Mass movement. This is far from what Dennis Fitzpatrick originally intended for his company. Liturgist George Devine (b. 1941) made the following observation:

> For Fitzpatrick, as for many new liturgical composers, [Ray Repp's popularity] signaled an ironic turn of events. Some of the work they had done that would be considered more "serious" or "substantial" would be ignored by the liturgical *aggiornamento*, like Fitzpatrick's *Demonstration English Mass*. Those who would survive in the field at all, like Fitzpatrick, would do so by adapting quickly to the vicissitudes of a wholly new "market" for liturgical music that would demand "Folk Mass" material almost as rapidly as it could be produced.
>
> What happened, between 1963 and 1967, was that the Church leap-frogged from a musical diet of *Missa Cantata* (solemn "High Mass"), with occasional English hymns for "Low Mass," to an infatuation with "Folk Mass" hymns, without stopping in between to consider the sung Mass at all seriously or thoroughly. This meant that Fitzpatrick and others who had prepared for the rendering of "High Mass" in English would find that they had been working on a product unwanted by most of the American Church. Under such circumstances, there would still be much use of the "Low Mass" hymns borrowed from the hymnals of our Protestant brothers, and even for some of the older pieces of music in the Catholic repertoire for choral and congregational use. But *Missa Cantata*, once vernacularized, seemed suddenly to die. Once removed from Rome in language, the American Church removed itself from Rome in ritual atmosphere as well, and the austere, the splendid, the solemn, the carefully executed all seemed to give way to the "pop," the streamlined, the "instant," the "funky."[18]

Ray Repp had kindled an entirely new fire. Although liturgical intellectuals felt a sense of loss, it seemed that American Catholics in the pews couldn't wait to "join in and sing."

1. Campbell, Joseph, with Moyers, Bill, *The Power of Myth* (New York: Doubleday, 1988) 84.
2. At this writing (2009), there is much discussion between Rome and the US Bishops on restoring the emphasis of chanting the prescribed entrance antiphon instead of singing a substitute entrance hymn.
3. Metrical markings are the numeric demarcation of the strong and weak accents in a given line of a hymn. "Hymnic literature has made use of poetic meter and rhythm resulting in a system of symbols and terminology peculiar to this area of study. An examination of any hymnal will reveal a metrical form indicated for most every hymn. Except for the three most frequently found meters — common, long and short — these will be shown in a series of digits: 8.7.8.7; 12.11.12.11; 7.7.7.7.7; for example." From Reynolds, William J. and Price, Milburn, *A Survey of Christian Hymnody* (Carol Stream, IL: Hope Publishing Co.) xv.
4. Interview with the author, March 6, 2004, Portland, Oregon, by phone to Shawano, Wisconsin.
5. Interview with the author, May 15, 2004, Las Vegas, Nevada.
6. That "someone" was Father (later Monsignor) Joe James, referenced in chapter 5 as the priest who made an informal recording of Repp's music during the 1965 summer orientation of the Extension Society program.
7. Interview with the author, October 1, 2004, Portland, Oregon, by phone to Ferrisburg, Vermont.
8. Ibid.
9. Liner notes (by Roger Nachtwey) from *Mass for Young Americans*.
10. Cook, Bruce, "How to Quit Fidgeting at Mass," *U.S. Catholic*, May 1967, 46.
11. FEL brochure, 1967.
12. Liner notes, *Paul Quinlan: Glory Bound*, LP album (America Record Society: 1965).
13. As will be seen in a later chapter, the *Hymnal for Young Christians* was a collection of the most prominent Folk Mass composers of the day.
14. Paul Quinlan will be profiled extensively in chapter 9.
15. There are two Anglican antecedents to the Repp Folk Mass worth mentioning: "'Twentieth Century Folk Mass' by Geoffrey Beaumont; sometimes mislabeled as a 'Jazz Mass,' this attempt was really something out of the 1940s movie musicals and generally dismissed as narrow in scope and superficial. Another work, by Anglican priest Ian Mitchell, was more in the traditional folk idiom of guitar music becoming popular on American campuses." From Devine, George, *Liturgical Renewal: An Agonizing Reappraisal* (Staten Island, NY: Alba House, 1973) 112. FEL later published Mitchell's Mass setting as "The American Folk-Song Mass."
16. Baptist John Fischer got his start on Repp's FEL label. See chapter 10.
17. Powell, Mark Allen, *Encyclopedia of Contemporary Christian Music* (Peabody, MA: Hendrickson Publishers, Inc., 2002) 751–752.
18. Devine, George, *Liturgical Renewal: An Agonizing Reappraisal* (Staten Island, NY: Alba House, 1973) 113–114.

Chapter Seven
"Wake Up, My People!"

Wake up, my people.
Wake up, give a shout!
Wake up, my people.
Know what life's about and

Wake up to the needs
of all the ones who suffer sorrow.
Wake up! Promise now
to do your best to change tomorrow.

Wake up, my people,
and open every door.
Wake up! It's time now:
Love my people evermore.[1]

—Ray Repp

The sound of a strumming guitar was as startling as Gabriel's trumpet, announcing not Judgment Day but, rather, an unforeseen awakening in the Roman liturgy. This was the revolution only hinted at in 1964. The change to the vernacular had been unsettling but interesting, and American Catholics grew into a gradual embrace of an English Mass that lifted the cloud of separation between the people and their beloved weekly ritual. No longer dependent on the need to silently follow the Latin with a loose English translation in their personal missals, Catholics began to relax with the new liturgy and slowly increased their level of active participation.

Then came the Folk Mass. You either loved it or hated it; there was no middle ground. Changing to English was one thing. Bringing guitars into the liturgy was another matter altogether. For some, particularly the young and the young at heart, the Folk Mass was the most exciting thing to happen to the Roman Catholic Church. For others, it was the last straw.

> An extraordinary night — and three minutes to midnight. But the Holy Cross [College] campus (Worcester, Massachusetts) looked like Homecoming. Boys with dates, and those without, hurried along, bellowing post-mortems about the day's football game, exams, and the weekly movie.

"What's all that noise?" yelled a shut-in from a dorm window.

> "It's Hallelujah Time," shouted a Crusader who knew.
>
> "Hallelujah Time" — that's what Holy Cross men call midnight Mass at the campus chapel, once a sanctuary for organ music and well-known hymns and now the launching ground for the Folk Mass...and a brilliant young man who is bringing new joyousness into the Church.
>
> Folk music's challenge to Brahms and the centuries-old form of worship in the Roman Catholic Church is the province of Paul Quinlan, a 28-year-old guitar-playing scholastic based at Holy Cross and regarded by the "swingers" as the "Jesuits' answer to the Singing Nun."[2]

Jan Coyle of Portland, Oregon, recalls her first Folk Mass. "I actually joined a group for a parish talent night called 'The Chanters' and it was in protest to the folk music that was coming. I was a 21-year-old dimwit who didn't know any better! But I was growing up, and my faith was growing, too. And the music was changing my mind.

"At the first Folk Mass I went to, I noticed that very few people left at Communion, and the whole vestibule was full of people talking after Mass. And I thought, 'This is great! This is wonderful!' And people were smiling in church. They were actually responding to the music and I realized that this is what the Church needed. It needed to have that door opened, the windows opened, to have some new life breathed into it. Within a couple of months I joined the folk group at Ascension Parish and have been there ever since. And we were down to grassroots where we were singing things like 'Get Together,' which was a secular song, and 'Love Come Trickling Down' [also known as 'Seek and Ye Shall Find'] because there was nothing much else to sing yet."[3]

> Remember the days when a student carrying a guitar was probably on his way to a hootenanny? Today it's possible he is on his way to take part in a Folk Mass.[4]

Pastoral musician Maureen Tauriello shares a familiar story. "I first experienced the Folk Mass in the '60s at our neighboring parish, Immaculate Heart of Mary in Maplewood, New Jersey. My home church — Our Lady of Sorrows in South Orange — was a very old, gothic-type place with no air conditioning. The new parish was created as a modern bright church with air conditioning, so in the summers our family would go there. They had a folk choir that was a multi-aged group — some adults and some kids — with four or five guitars, an occasional tambourine, and maybe a bongo. I loved it! The songs were so bright and easy to sing, they seemed 'cool' as opposed to the stuffy hymns at my home church. The guitars played in unison, nothing fancy. When I sang along in the pews, I felt like dancing and clapping. It was a joyful experience."[5]

> One priest said, "Young people in my parish are overwhelmingly 'for' the guitar Mass. It is my firm conviction that the new music fills a special need for youth."

> A 19-year-old music major at a Catholic college said, "The Mass has become a more profound religious experience for me because of the new music. Older people don't seem to realize that there are many paths to God."[6]

Seventh grader Bruce Bruno (b. 1960) was sitting in the playground of Our Lady of Victory School in Cincinnati, Ohio, with his pals, Scott and Cindy. They regularly spent their recess time together, often with pencil and paper, as if doing homework. But they also had guitars, and soon Bill, the fourth member of their clique, would come running toward them.

"Hey, guys! Listen to this!" Bill said breathlessly as he sat down next to Bruce on the curb and grabbed his friend's guitar. He launched into a halting but enthusiastic rendition of a new Ray Repp song called "To Be Alive." The other kids sang and strummed along immediately. At the tender age of 12, Bruce, Bill, Scott, and Cindy were the leaders of their parish school's Folk Mass group and they were constantly looking for new songs, copying down each other's discoveries on scribbled manuscript paper at every free moment. This new Repp song was just what they needed for the entrance song for their Wednesday morning school Mass. The parish's forward-thinking principal had no hesitation about entrusting music leadership to these talented youngsters.

At the next school liturgy, Bruce's father, Ray Bruno (1936–1998), could only smile proudly in the congregation as his son strummed and sang his heart out with his buddies. Bruno was general manager of World Library of Sacred Music, and young Bruce was a chip off the old block.[7]

> Young people all over the country all seem to be enthusiastic about the *idea* of the Folk Mass; and those who actually take part are soon deeply committed to the movement. At Loyola University in Chicago, attendance at the chapel is up appreciably since they began to experiment with guitar Masses there last fall. Yes, this can rightfully be called a movement, all right, for it has behind it not only the raw, spontaneous enthusiasm of the young, but the considered approbation of many liturgists and theologians.[8]

Medical Mission Sister Miriam Therese Winter (b. 1938) has this recollection in her autobiography.

> I was told that I would study sacred music. Talk of a Vatican Council and rumors of significant change had convinced my major superiors that someone would have to be prepared to help the sisters navigate the turbulent waters that lay ahead. So I studied sacred music — organ, polyphony, chant — directed our community choirs, and graduated from The Catholic University with a bachelor's degree in music.
>
> Within months after I received my degree in the traditional Latin heritage

of the universal Church, the vernacular language became mandatory for the celebration of the liturgy throughout the United States. With the loss of Latin went the core of my training and the clarity of my call.

I was assigned to teach novices at the motherhouse in Philadelphia, a task I took up with a heavy heart, extinguishing that final flicker of hope for a mission overseas. Discouraged, disillusioned, struggling to accept the inevitable and unwilling to walk away, I picked up a guitar that had been lying around and taught myself some chords. It was, after all, the Sixties. Folk music was everywhere. Influenced by its accessible sound and narrative capacity, I climbed to the crest of a rolling hill where the sky reaches to the horizon, and I began to sing.

It was a match made in heaven, the wedding of word to a singable song, and it was life-giving for me. To sing discontent into meaning became a source of survival and therapy for the heart.

> I saw raindrops on my window.
> Joy is like the rain.
> Laughter runs across my pain,
> slips away and comes again.
> Joy is like the rain...[9]

The Folk Mass was captured in popular literature.

> There is a singing group in this Catholic church today, a singing group which calls itself "Wildflowers." The lead is a tall, square-jawed teen-aged boy, buoyant and glad to be here. He carries a guitar; he plucks out a little bluesy riff and hits some chords. With him are the rest of the Wildflowers. There is an old woman, wonderfully determined; she has orange hair and is dressed country-and-western style. A long embroidered strap around her neck slings a big western guitar low over her pelvis. Beside her stands a frail, withdrawn fourteen-year-old boy, and a large Chinese man in his twenties who seems to enjoy himself but is not quite sure how to. He looks around wildly as he sings, and shuffles his feet. There is also a very tall teen-aged girl, presumably the lead singer's girlfriend; she is delicate of feature, half-serene and petrified, a wispy soprano. They straggle out in front of the altar and teach us a brand new hymn...[10]

Social justice advocate Dorothy Day (1897–1980) wrote about the phenomenon.

> [This] leads me into reflections on the new Masses, the intimate Masses, the colloquial Masses, the folk-song Masses, and so on. By the intimate I mean those where everyone gathers close around the altar inside the sanctuary, as close to the priest as possible. By the intimate I also mean those offered in small apartments before a small group. I understand that permission for this has been granted in Harlem for some time now, and

> priests are offering Mass in the poorest of homes block by block in their parishes, during the week — bringing Christ most literally to the people. This is wonderful.
>
> I do love the guitar Masses, the Masses where the recorder and the flute are played, and sometimes the glorious and triumphant trumpet. But I do not want them every day, any more than we ever wanted solemn Gregorian Requiem Masses every day. They are for the occasion. The guitar Masses I have heard from one end of the country to the other are all different and have a special beauty of their own. I have been a participant (it is not that I have just heard them) in such Masses with the Franciscan Brothers in Santa Barbara, with the students at St. Louis University, at the McGill Newman Club in Montreal, and many other Newman meetings, and in Barrytown, New York, where the Christian Brothers, our neighbors, have a folk Mass every Saturday at eleven-fifteen. They are joyful and happy Masses indeed and supposed to attract the young. But the beginning of faith is something different. "The *fear* of the Lord is the beginning of wisdom." Fear in the sense of *awe*.[11]

Marie Phillippi, former workshop coordinator of Oregon Catholic Press (OCP), remembers: "I was a very, very young nun, and my first assignment was to teach grade school music three days a week at Saint Ignatius, the Jesuit parish in Portland. In 1967, our pastor, Father McHugh, decided that we needed to get going on the music to bring the young people back to Church. And so he asked Jeannie Rae Routtu, a wonderful musician, to start and lead the folk group.

"Father McHugh would come out of the sacristy 15 to 20 minutes before Mass because people were coming in early and talking. And they would sing and he would pray a little bit with them. Folks were standing in the aisles and sitting on the floor in the front. The church was packed. I just watched for six months and I saw how it grew and grew until it was people of all ages. It wasn't just the young. The older people loved it. They came in early. So eventually I told Jeannie that I would be glad to sing and play something. Well, I got to do the percussion. I played a little glockenspiel and the tambourine. And the folk group was right up in front, whereas the choir always had the organ in the back."[12]

> The strumming of guitars, like the Pied Piper, continues to woo students to Mass. At the Saint Meinrad School of Theology [Indiana], 19 deacons presented a Folk Mass for high school students. Almost half of the 380 students attended the non-compulsory "Whoozit" and were high in their praise of the approach. Said a priest, "I would never have tried it. It sounded corny to me at first, but I was mistaken. The kids loved it."[13]

Liturgical composer Janèt Sullivan Whitaker (b. 1958) has these Folk Mass memories: "By the time I was 10, my family was fully involved in the music of the Folk Mass. There were guitars, bass, drums, and a lot of secular songs with reworked lyrics.

There wasn't a lot of music available, so we came up with our own as best we could. My father, Tom Sullivan (b. 1932), did a lot with re-writing pop songs like The Sandpipers' 'Guantanamera' and 'Love Train' by the O'Jays.

"I knew the music of Ray Repp from Catholic school student Masses. My early favorites were 'I Am the Resurrection' and 'Peace, My Friends.' I still love those songs. I remember some Folk Mass songs were hokey. Even when they were new, I found them trite and somewhat embarrassing. For better or worse, it was definitely a blast of fresh air to have the new music.

"My family belonged to Saint Edward Church in Newark, California. My brothers and sisters and I attended the Catholic school in that parish, which is part of the Oakland Diocese, located in the East Bay of the San Francisco area.

"Involvement was compulsory for the Sullivan family. I was one of eleven musical siblings, and my dad insisted we all be a part of the music at those liturgies. It was not an option. My older brothers and my sister Anna all played band instruments at the Sunday Masses. I played a little bit of guitar, but mostly sang with my family. I played piano and led singing at school liturgies and parish funerals from about the age of eleven until I went on to high school. I remember playing 'You'll Never Walk Alone,' 'Those Who See Light.' the Beatles' 'Let It Be,' and 'Let There Be Peace on Earth' at liturgy.

"My father was one of the first lay people to serve on the diocesan music sub-committee, which was formed to facilitate the implementation of liturgical music reforms. He was very active in all aspects of the change at our parish: from tearing out the Communion rails to squaring off with the old-school ushers who hated all the music. It was a tumultuous time. There was much shouting and many angry words. The liturgical reforms — indeed the principles of the liturgy as the work of the people — were constant topics of discussion around our family dinner table. I learned the words 'full, conscious, and active participation' well before I could comprehend them or even spell all the words. It was part of my life."[14]

> Bishop Flanagan of Worcester, Massachusetts, has granted permission to the students of Assumption College for a weekly Mass accompanied by guitars. One student remarked: "The most important aspect of this type of Mass is that it reaches all who attend — or rather assist — because everyone participates fully, even the older people who say they really gain something spiritually from this great degree of participation.[15]

Mercy Sister Suzanne Toolan (b. 1927), renowned for her timeless hymn, "I Am the Bread of Life," was already an accomplished organist in the 1950s and '60s, having studied with organ maestro Richard Key Biggs when she was in high school. Here is her reaction to the Folk Mass.

"I have to say I welcomed the folk-style music at Mass. Not all of it was really good, but there was a freshness about it. And it was so important for young people, because they were already not getting involved. I remember being on the liturgical commission in San Francisco and we were trying to get some of the hierarchy in the archdiocese to realize that they had to do something for youth. So I remember that at this particular meeting we set it up so that we brought some young people in to talk to them and, oh, they would say exactly what they felt. I remember one of the old priests saying, 'Well, not going to Mass — don't you know that's a mortal sin?' And one young person responded, 'Hey, man, the mortal sin is on you for boring me!' Such honesty!

"I wrote for organ but I liked to hear my songs on guitar. I thought it was great. Sometimes the rhythms wouldn't be so great, but when I heard my songs with guitar, and with trumpets added, it was very nice. And I even tried to learn the guitar by myself. So I found an empty room and I said, 'I'm not going to appear a learner. I'm going to come out full-blown.' So I struggled along and after a week or so I decided I couldn't do it. So I never learned guitar.

"In the 60s, spontaneity was much needed, to create a sense of informality that was just not possible in the old structure. The Folk Mass was more spontaneous and seemed to honor enthusiasm. That was a lovely thing. But it didn't have a lot of grounding. That wouldn't come until many years later."[16]

> Aided by three guitars and 12,000 foot-tapping schoolchildren, the Roman Catholic Archbishop of New York transformed the Central Park Mall into a festive outdoor cathedral yesterday.
>
> The Most. Rev. Terence J. Cooke [1921–1983], dressed in red Episcopal robes and wearing a gold mitre, led what Chancery officials said was the first Mass to be held in the park. It was also one of the few times that an American Bishop has led a folk or guitar Mass.
>
> Handmade banners in multicolored felt and burlap gave a psychedelic air to the concrete bandstand. A pink and yellow one proclaimed the theme of the day: "United in Him. We Sing with Joy." A green one said simply: "We love. We live."
>
> Three students from Cathedral College, the archdiocesan minor seminary, took their guitars and began strumming the bouncy refrain that has become the staple of folk Masses:
>
> "Sons of God, hear his holy word...."[17]

Of course, not everyone was enamored of the Folk Mass movement. Liturgical music critic Thomas Day (b. 1943), no relation to Dorothy Day, has his own recollection of those times.

> I can remember attending those first parish "Folk Masses" back in the 1960s, when the liturgy was partly in Latin and partly in English. Most of the people seemed to be having a grand time. At the Entrance they

sang "Michael, Row the Boat Ashore." At the Offertory there was "Kumbaya." Communion featured "Sons of God" (with the happy-go-lucky refrain, "Eat his body, drink his blood. Allelu!"). Hands clapped. Guitars twanged. A somewhat nervous clergy, not quite sure of what it should do with the folk believers, often put them "downstairs" in the basement church. The "upstairs" church would be reserved for the "regular" liturgy. Back in those days all signs indicated that nothing would stop the "downstairs" revolution — not even its own excesses, its very own innocent blasphemies.

Who could ever forget those three-chord guitarists! They certainly gave another dimension of meaning to the word "monotonous." Communion meditations became interminable exercises in self-pity. Members of the folk group would sometimes tell little stories or jokes before each song; sometimes they would have arguments about the music while the priest and congregation watched and waited. It was considered so very natural, so very much in the folk style when a mother and father, two singers in a folk group, changed their baby's fully loaded diaper right in front of the congregation (so help me!).

If someone ever gives a prize for conspicuous vulgarity, above and beyond the call of duty, I would like to nominate one especially inept parish folk group in Connecticut. While the congregation tried to follow the actions of the Mass, the women in this ensemble — they wore tight clam-digger pants — would writhe in a kind of heated agitation, directly in front of the congregation, and slap tambourines against their ample buttocks, in time with the music.[18]

Folk Masses were inevitably banned by those in authority.

In Milwaukee, Archbishop William E. Cousins [1902–1988] has forbidden the use of guitars, drums, and secular music. "Spirituals and similar songs, including popular hit tunes, religious parodies on folk tunes, jazz and the like do not conform to the requirements for liturgical music."

Bishop Maurice Schexnayder [1895–1981] of Lafayette, Louisiana has also issued an unequivocal ban on the use of jazz and folk music in church.[19]

Sister Germaine Habjan (b. 1944), who carved out an impressive career as a Folk Mass composer, lived as a student with fellow Glenmary sisters at Marquette University in the Archdiocese of Milwaukee. Her college Folk Mass experience reflected the inherent tensions between the sacred and the secular.

Recently, the sisters were saddened because the use of folk music in the liturgy was forbidden by the bishop of Milwaukee as "unsuited" for worship. On Sunday mornings, nevertheless, Marquette students crowd into the dining room and living room of their Glenmary apartment for the Eucharist, and for coffee and rolls afterward. The eight attractive, talented sisters are not afraid to "mix with seculars," but feel strengthened thereby in their service of God's people.[20]

Ray Orrock (1929–2008), a California columnist for the *Oakland Tribune*, penned a tongue-in-cheek parody called "A Traditionalist's Lament," sung to the tune of the popular *Mary Poppins* song, "Supercalifragilisticexpialadocious."

> Refrain:
> Intriobo. Tantum Ergo. Kyrie Eleison.
> Give me back my pamphlet rack and surplices with lace on.
> If Catholic means rock-and-roll I'd rather be a Mason.
> Introibo. Tantum Ergo. Kyrie Eleison.
>
> I used to sing of Christ the King and goodly saints of yore,
> But now some fool named Michael tries to row the boat ashore.
> The Father, Son and Holy Ghost have given way to trash.
> The Trinity has been replaced by Crosby, Stills and Nash. (refrain)[21]

Although Orrock wrote this for a 1969 seminar on humor, many a traditionalist got a kick out it, especially the final stanza that outlined his funeral plans: "as I soar to heaven's door to rest among the stars, please bear me there with angel harps, not banjos and guitars!"

> In Detroit, the archdiocesan music commission has banned Father Ian Mitchell's *An American Folk-Song Mass,* explaining that both the words and music "violate the rules" laid down for church music.[22]

As publisher of *Mass for Young Americans, An American Folk-Song Mass,* and other emerging folk music for liturgy, classical composer Dennis Fitzpatrick (b. 1937) ironically became the staunchest defender of the Folk Mass, making himself available for numerous interviews.

> Fitzpatrick was quite frank in discussing the widespread and hard-necked opposition with which the very idea of the sung English Mass was met in the beginning. "Not *just* the idea of the Guitar or Folk Mass," he emphasized. "For instance, there is the much different approach of Father Clarence Rivers. His is a Mass which makes strong use of the Negro spiritual style in its approach. It is very much in the American idiom in this way. Immediately after the English translation of the Mass was published in 1964, Father Rivers, who had been working on his Mass for quite some time, had it introduced. And it was immediately banned in several dioceses, San Francisco and others more or less liberal among them. Banned — I want to make this clear — virtually without a hearing, just on principle alone."

Asked about other dioceses around the country, he said that Milwaukee had probably been the bitterest opponent to the movement. "There," he said, "they banned music in the folk and jazz idioms in church as *categories*. There was no attempt to judge individual works on their own merits, just a flat refusal to listen.

"It's true enough that for years young people's worship was completely ignored. But now, of course, we've seen the tremendous success this folk idiom has had with the young, so we assume — well, of course, it's for high school and college students, nothing more. But those who are actually presenting and participating in the Folk Mass are finding out that the response of adults is the same. They are, in many parishes and situations, just as enthusiastic as the young people. Once they overcome a sort of initial shyness, they chime in just as loud as the rest. Let's face it: this is *American* music, not just American high school music."[23]

Was the Folk Mass just a fad, to be tolerated only for the sake of getting young people more involved in church? What was the official word from the United States Bishops? Did they approve? Or was participation in a Folk Mass considered an act of disobedience?

In the 1960s, did anybody really care about disobedience?

---

1 "Wake Up, My People" ©1967, Otter Creek Music. Published by OCP. All rights reserved.
2 Collins, Pat, "Swinging Jesuit: Priest-to-Be at Holy Cross Answer to 'Singing Nun,'" *Coloroto Magazine* (Sunday supplement to the *New York Daily News*), January 22, 1967.
3 Interview with the author, May 26, 2004, Portland, Oregon.
4 Rudcki, Rev. Stanley R., "Sing a New Song to the Lord," *Extension*, August 1966, 29.
5 Interview with the author, January 30, 2007.
6 Shanahan, Louise, "Music at Mass: Where Is It Going?" *Catholic Home*, October 1968, 14.
7 Interview with the author, February 10, 2007, Beaverton, Oregon.
8 Cook, Bruce, "How to Quit Fidgeting at Mass," *U.S. Catholic*, May 1967, 43.
9 Winter, Miriam Therese, *The Singer and the Song: An Autobiography of the Spirit* (Maryknoll, New York: Orbis Books, 1999) 4–6.
10 Dillard, Annie, *Teaching a Stone to Talk* (New York: Harper and Row, 1982) 17–18.
11 Day, Dorothy, *On Pilgrimage* (Grand Rapids: William B. Eerdmans Publishing Co., 1999) 38–39.
12 Interview with the author, September 27, 2004, Portland, Oregon.
13 Rudcki, Rev. Stanley R., "Sing a New Song to the Lord," *Extension*, August 1966, 31.
14 Interview with the author, January 26, 2007, from Hayward, California.
15 Rudcki, Rev. Stanley R., "Sing a New Song to the Lord," *Extension*, August 1966, 31.
16 Interview with the author, July 21, 2005, at Mercy Center, Burlingame, CA.
17 "Park Becomes Cathedral for 12,000," *New York Times*, May 7, 1968.
18 Day, Thomas, *Why Catholics Can't Sing: The Culture of Catholicism and the Triumph of Bad Taste* (New York: Crossroad Publishing Company, 1990) 58–59.
19 Rudcki, Rev. Stanley R., "Sing a New Song to the Lord," *Extension*, August 1966, 30.
20 "The New Nuns," *Saturday Evening Post*, July 30, 1966.
21 Burns, Jeffrey M., and Batiza, Mary Carmen, *We Are the Church: A History of the Diocese of Oakland* (Strasbourg, France: Editions du Signe, 2001) 53.
22 Rudcki, Rev. Stanley R., "Sing a New Song to the Lord," *Extension*, August 1966, 30.
23 Cook, Bruce, "How to Quit Fidgeting at Mass," *U.S. Catholic*, May 1967, 46.

Glenmary Sister Germaine Habjan

Ray Repp

The Dameans

Dave Baker, Darryl Ducote, Mike Balhoff, Buddy Ceasar, and Gary Ault.

(Unless otherwise noted, photos are courtesy of Dennis Fitzpatrick)

Roger Nachtwey, Demonstration English Mass

Joe Wise
(Photo courtesy of GIA Publications, Inc.)

Jack Miffleton

Carey Landry

(Unless otherwise noted, photos are courtesy of Dennis Fitzpatrick)

Dennis Fitzpatrick

John Fischer

Sebastian Temple
(OCP photo)

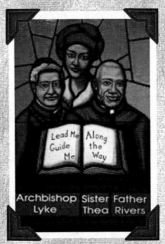

Archbishop James Lyke, OFM;
Sr. Thea Bowman, FSPA;
Father Clarence Rivers
(Photo courtesy of Holy Redeemer Church, San Antonio, Texas.)

The Paul Quinlan Trio

Rich Regan, Paul Quinlan, and Steve Seery.

Bob Hurd

Peter Scholtes (on guitar) and unidentified members of the St. Brendan Choir.

(Unless otherwise noted, photos are courtesy of Dennis Fitzpatrick)

Chapter Eight
Hymnal for Young Christians

> DETROIT, Jan. 31 (AP) — A group of University of Detroit students demonstrated yesterday in front of the Archdiocese of Detroit Chancery against a ban of a folk-music-style Mass.
>
> The ban came hours earlier in the form of a letter from Chancery officials read to students and faculty gathered to hear the Mass in the Student Union building.
>
> Some 50 students marched in freezing weather in front of the Chancery, carrying a sign: "We want our Mass."
>
> The ban was signed by the director of the archdiocesan music commission. It said the folk-music Mass — performed with guitar music — "didn't quite meet the standards of liturgical music."[1]
>
> —*New York Times*

Although the Folk Mass sometimes became a worshipful act of defiance in dioceses that banned it, conscientious pastors and musicians preferred to celebrate these liturgies with some sort of official approval. The Bishops' Commission on the Liturgical Apostolate[2] was entrusted with the responsibility to oversee liturgical reform. They wasted no time issuing guidelines for the Folk Mass movement that was spreading across the country like wildfire.

Issued on April 18, 1966, and simply titled "Church Music," the statement gave directives on celebrating a Folk Mass without actually using that name. By sandwiching the topic between guidelines on the role of the choir and a discussion on the salaries of Church musicians, the Commission deliberately framed its instruction so as not to give the Folk Mass any more attention than it deemed necessary. While certainly a hot topic of the day, the Folk Mass was considered by most liturgists as a fad that was pertinent only to "a particular age group" — youth — not a general parish assembly. The Commission had other important liturgical priorities to manage, including the question of concelebration, Communion under both species, and the unauthorized liturgical experimentation that was beginning to surface.

> In modern times, the Church has consistently recognized and freely admitted the use of various styles of music as an aid to liturgical worship. Since the promulgation of the *Constitution on the Liturgy,* and more especially since the introduction of vernacular languages into the liturgy, there has arisen a more pressing need for musical composition in idioms that can be sung by the congregation and thus further communal participation.

Experience has, furthermore, shown that different groupings of the faithful assembled in worship respond to different styles of musical expression which help to make the liturgy meaningful for them. Thus, the needs of the faithful of a particular cultural background or of a particular age level may often be met by a music that can serve as a congenial, liturgically oriented expression of prayer.

In this connection, when a service of worship is conducted primarily for gatherings of youth of high school or college age, and not for ordinary congregations, the choice of music which is meaningful to persons of this age level should be considered valid and purposeful.

The use of this [new] music presupposes:

a) that the music itself can be said to contain genuine merit;

b) that if instruments other than the organ are employed as accompaniment for the singing, they should be played in a manner that is suitable for public worship;

c) that the liturgical texts should be respected. The incorporation of incongruous melodies and texts, adapted from popular ballads, should be avoided.[3]

There has been much retrospective discussion of the alleged "railroading" of this statement through the Commission-at-large by a small handful of progressive members. Susan Benofy, of the traditional Adoremus group, provides this account.

A Music Advisory Board was formed in 1965 to assist [the Commission on the Liturgical Apostolate]. At its first meeting in Detroit in May 1965, Benedictine Archabbot Rembert Weakland (later Archbishop of Milwaukee) was elected chairman and (then) Father Richard Schuler, Secretary. [Father] McManus was the official liaison with the bishops.

At its February 1966 meeting, the Music Advisory Board was presented with a proposal for the use of guitars and folk music in the liturgy. Monsignor Schuler gives an account of the meeting:

It was clear at the meeting that both Father McManus and Archabbot Weakland were most anxious to obtain the board's approval.... Vigorous debate considerably altered the original proposal, and a much modified statement about "music for special groups" was finally approved by a majority of one, late in the day when many members had already left.[4]

No matter how the statement was crafted, it was published with the weight and authority of the Commission of the Liturgical Apostolate on behalf of the US Bishops.

This was good enough for most dioceses, although many took it upon themselves to promulgate additional guidelines for their local churches. The Archdiocese of San Francisco issued such a statement on October 3, 1966:

1. In the Archdiocese of San Francisco, "instruments other than the organ" include all *non-electric string instruments.*

2. This type of music may not be used for "ordinary parish congregations."

3. The music used at Mass should be a genuine and a sensible prayer.

4. The words should be related as closely as possible to the parts of the Mass during which they are sung.

5. Instruments other than the organ should be played in such a way as to provide a very reverent and harmonious background accompaniment for really religious music. They should never be played in such a manner as to excite feelings that might be inappropriate at Mass.

6. The Bishops have stated that the "incorporation of incongruous melodies and texts, adapted from popular ballads, should be avoided." This would refer to the use of such melodies as "Michael Row Your Boat Ashore," "If I Had a Hammer," "500 Miles," "The Tune from Exodus," "Puff, the Magic Dragon," "The Whistling Gypsy," "Blowin' in the Wind," etc.

7. The folk idiom must never be used exclusively as music for worship by these special groups. There should be a mixture of both conventional and folk elements.

8. These experiments must be conducted with the approval of the administrators involved, e.g., school principal, and after consultation with competent musicians and liturgists.[5]

The directives of the Archdiocese of San Francisco, a politically liberal city, seemed especially strict, with little or no wiggle room for musical creativity. One is reminded of the stereotypical pre-Vatican II Catholic high school dance, when the principal would address the teenagers in the gymnasium before the music started, reminding them of the virtues of chastity and the pains of hell. Having filled their young minds with unpleasant images of eternal damnation, Father would then smile slightly and say to his students, "Well, have a good time!"

The San Francisco directives were in marked contrast to what was happening across the bay in the Diocese of Oakland, where Father E. Donald Osuna (b. 1936) was appointed in 1967 by Bishop Floyd L. Begin (1902–1977) to take charge of the liturgies at Saint Francis de Sales Cathedral with the specific goal of "creating a model of

Vatican II liturgy." The parish committed more than 25% of its resources to support the liturgy, but they still could not purchase a new organ. Instead, Osuna formed an ensemble that consisted of strings, brass, piano, guitar, and other instruments.[6]

> The ensemble performed songs that ranged from classical to pop and created what came to be known as the "Oakland Cathedral Sound," which soon garnered national attention. In May 1971, *Time* magazine observed, "twice each Sunday, the music runs the scale between such unlikely extremes as Gregorian chant and rock. On one recent Sunday, the mixture embraced both Bach's "Air on the G-String" and "Amazing Grace." On another, it included a Haydn trio, Bob Dylan's "The Times They Are a-Changin'" and Luther's "A Mighty Fortress Is Our God." Worshippers came from all over the Bay Area. The music also attempted to reflect the ethnic make-up of the parish. Soon Negro spirituals and Spanish hymns were featured regularly.[7]

As word got out, the Oakland cathedral liturgies were packed with standing-room-only crowds of worshippers from around the diocese and throughout North America. In addition to musical excellence, Osuna and his liturgists incorporated innovations in art, drama, dance, photography, and compelling preaching. When the Federation of Diocesan Liturgical Commissions (FDLC) held its national convention in San Francisco in 1971, they celebrated their principal liturgy at Saint Francis de Sales Cathedral, much to the embarrassment of the host archdiocese which had just dedicated its own modern Saint Mary's Cathedral. FDLC organizers informed Osuna: "We want to worship with your people, in your space, which all of us agree is the most exciting in the country."[8]

In fairness to the Church in San Francisco, at least Folk Masses were permitted. Further down the coast, the Archdiocese of Los Angeles effectively banned such liturgies for three years until their Music Commission issued its own guidelines in 1969.

To guide the parishes in their choice of music Father (later Monsignor) Robert Hayburn (d. 1991), San Francisco's Music Commission chairman, included with the archdiocesan directive "a list of available music, including such items as *Hymnal for Young Christians,* published by the Friends of the English Liturgy at Chicago, Illinois."[9]

• ■ •

The phone in the FEL office was ringing off the hook, even as mountains of unsolicited tapes and manuscripts were piled high on Roger Nachtwey's desk. The success of *Mass for Young Americans* opened the floodgates. Suddenly, anybody who could play four chords on the guitar decided they could also write music for liturgy, and why not? All one needed were simple chords, a catchy melody, and heartfelt, uplifting lyrics. That formula worked for Ray Repp. Why couldn't it work for others? Unfortunately, most of the unsolicited music was unsingable, and a standard rejection letter was issued.

> After careful consideration, the FEL music review board has decided to return your materials. Although we feel your work has merit, it does not meet the needs of our current publishing schedule....[10]

The "music review board" was basically one person, Nachtwey himself. After an initial screening, Nachtwey would forward worthy possibilities to Fitzpatrick for final approval. Occasionally, additional input was provided by FEL staffers Thomas Cook (b. 1938) and Fran Farber. A few years later, Jim Schaefer (d. 1980s) would formally assume the FEL music review process as Director of Artists and Repertoire.

Hymnal for Young Christians, chosen as the company's primary follow-up to Ray Repp's *Mass for Young Americans,* was a collection of folk hymns by composers from around the country. Over the next year, the FEL staff busied itself with the necessary steps of song reviewing, talent scouting, record production, music engraving, and aggressive promotion.

In 1966, Catholic publishers found themselves facing an unprecedented problem: a clamor for a product that had not even existed six months previously. Repp's debut album, released in February, created excitement, but it had only ten songs plus a Mass setting. As Folk Masses began to be celebrated weekly, musicians wanted to do more than just sing "Sons of God" and "Here We Are" every Sunday. Composers Joe Wise (b. 1939), Paul Quinlan, Sister Germaine Habjan, and Father Peter Scholtes (b. 1938) were writing and performing remarkable songs at their local liturgies, but the official publication and national distribution of their music was months away.

In the meantime, parish folk choirs had no choice but to rely on secular sources to keep their weekly repertoire fresh. Although the liturgy guidelines of San Francisco and other dioceses reacted against this trend, for young people it seemed quite natural to sing their favorite secular music at a Folk Mass, especially songs with a spiritual bent. Pete Seeger's (b. 1919) "If I Had a Hammer" was a terrific entrance song for a liturgy that focused on social justice. Bob Dylan's (b. 1941) "Blowing in the Wind" captured a generation's questioning and fit perfectly at the offertory, bringing such questions to the altar along with the gifts of bread and wine.

Admittedly, this sometimes became a stretch. What place did "Michael Row the Boat Ashore" have as a Communion song? At least "Kum Ba Yah" was a prayer that actually mentions the Lord. But did anyone really know the meaning behind the words *kum ba yah*?

Thoughtful priests and music leaders knew that the music for Mass had to at least be meaningful. "Puff, the Magic Dragon" had no place in the liturgy, no matter how much a homilist might try to impose a Christian message behind the actions of Little Jackie Paper. So, in the grand tradition of secular folk music, Folk Mass singers simply changed the words of popular songs to fit the circumstances of the liturgy. The refrain to Dylan's "Blowing in the Wind" was often rendered as: "The answer, my friend, is living in our midst...."

There was an illegal songbook that was wildly popular on the West Coast entitled *Happiness Is a Song.* Published cheaply and anonymously, with neither composer nor publisher credits, the songbook contained the lyrics and chords to over 300 of the most trendy folk and pop songs of the day, including the works of the Kingston Trio; Peter, Paul & Mary; Bob Dylan; Simon & Garfunkel; and many others. It also contained liturgical lyrics for many of these secular songs, giving weight to the rumor that *Happiness Is a Song* was the underground handiwork of an unnamed California seminary. Here are two examples of liturgical adaptation from the songbook.

"One in Him"
(sung to the melody of "Five Hundred Miles")

One in life, one in love, one in him who reigns above,
We are all one family, one in love.

(Chorus)
Thy kingdom come, thy kingdom come,
thy kingdom come, thy will be done.
We are all one family, one in love.

In one bread, in one wine, we the branches, he the vine,
He has made us one in him, who is divine. (Chorus)

To the Father, to the Son, to the Spirit, Three-in-One,
Now let all creation sing, "Thy will be done." (Chorus)

"Gather Christians"
(sung to the melody of "Michael, Row the Boat Ashore")

Gather, Christians, to hear his Word, alleluia,
And eat the banquet of the Lord, alleluia.

In joyful song our voices raise, alleluia.
To God above we offer praise, alleluia.

As one body with Christ, our head, alleluia,
The People of God will share one bread, alleluia.

Now with one voice we join to sing, alleluia,
In love and honor to our King, alleluia.[11]

Lyric adaptation was an inadequate solution to the thin Folk Mass repertoire. The popular melodies enabled congregations to sing immediately, but no matter how liturgical the new words were, the secular connotations always came to mind. One couldn't help but to think about "hearing the whistle blow" while singing an adaptation of "Five Hundred Miles" at Mass. Meanwhile, pastors and parish music leaders prayed that the Catholic publishers would come out with new material quickly.

As *Hymnal for Young Christians* neared completion, Fitzpatrick scored a coup by obtaining a notable endorsement.

> The compilers of this collection have taken up the challenge of Vatican II to search for meaningful and new modes of expressing man's love of God and of neighbor.
>
> As truly American as the pioneer spirit it implies, this group of hymns and songs for young people represents one possible avenue for this quest, particularly in catechetical work and liturgical ceremonies, and as such receives the approbation of the Music Division of the Liturgical Commission, Diocese of Sioux Falls, South Dakota, August 15, 1966.[12]

While not really a bishop's *imprimatur*,[13] Fitzpatrick pasted the endorsement onto *HYC*'s cover page and trumpeted it widely in the book's promotions as an "ecclesiastical approbation." After all, FEL was treading into uncertain waters with the very concept of a hymnal that would exclusively serve the Folk Mass movement.

In terms of sales, the endorsement proved helpful to musicians who needed to justify the new resource to their pastors. Released in January 1967, *Hymnal for Young Christians* was an immediate hit, necessitating a second printing in May of that year, and a third in August, to meet the demand for the Liturgical Week conference in Kansas City. Copies of *HYC* were flying out of the FEL exhibit during the conference, and an impromptu late-night sing-along at the booth drew the ire of convention center officials who were trying in vain to clear the large crowd so they could close the venue for the night.

Certainly, *Hymnal for Young Christians* was ambitious, comprising seven Mass settings, 35 psalm settings, and 172 songs written by over 16 composers. *HYC* was on the bookshelf of just about every parish and campus music office, and a church musician was considered cool if it was part of his or her collection of accompaniment books. Enthusiasts of the Folk Mass movement were enthralled to have in one resource *Mass for Young Americans*, all their favorite Repp songs, the dynamic new hymn "They'll Know We Are Christians," and so much more. With over 300 pages, there was a wealth of new songs and new composers to discover. The Jesuit magazine, *America*, gave a quick endorsement to FEL's new works.

> A new *Missa Bossa Nova*, hailing from Chicago's South Side, is available from FEL Church Publications and holds some pleasant surprises for you. FEL now has a Second *Mass for Young Americans* by Ray Repp, on a jubilant release called *Allelu!* and another new record with Sister Germaine's beguiling *Songs of Salvation*. Words and music of all this material, as well as hymns and psalms by Paul Quinlan, Clarence Rivers, and Robert Blue are published in FEL's new *Hymnal for Young Christians*. Chaplains and others who work with youth would do well to look into this attractive hymnal.[14]

So many new Folk Mass composers! Who were these singing young Christians?

1 "Detroit U. Students Protest Ban on Folk-Music Mass," *New York Times*, February 1, 1966.
2 The Commission for the Liturgical Apostolate came to be known as the Bishops' Committee on the Liturgy (BCL). The Liturgy Secretariat is now known as the Committee on Divine Worship (CDW).
3 McManus, Frederick R., editor, *Thirty Years of Liturgical Renewal: Statements of the Bishops' Committee on the Liturgy* (Washington, DC: United States Catholic Conference, Inc., 1987) 44.
4 Benofy, Susan, "Buried Treasure: Can the Church Recover Her Musical Heritage?" *Adoremus Bulletin*, Vol. VII, No. 3: May 2001.
5 Hayburn, Rev. Robert F., "To Pray In Beauty: Music for Special Groups," *Musart: Official Publication of the National Catholic Music Educators Association*, Volume XX, Number 1, September–October 1967, 33–34.
6 Osuna was also a Folk Mass composer. His most famous song, "Those Who See Light," is still being sung at liturgy in 2009.
7 Burns, Jeffrey M., and Batiza, Mary Carmen, *We Are the Church: A History of the Diocese of Oakland* (Strasbourg, France: Editions du Signe, 2001) 51–53.
8 Ibid., 54.
9 Hayburn, Rev. Robert F., "To Pray In Beauty: Music for Special Groups," *Musart: Official Publication of the National Catholic Music Educators Association*, Volume XX, Number 1, September-October 1967, 34.
10 Standard FEL rejection letter for unsolicited music.
11 No composer credits were given in the *Happiness Is a Song* book. After all, it was illegal.
12 *Hymnal for Young Christians*, FEL Publications, Ltd., First Printing, January 1967.
13 An *imprimatur* is an official declaration from the hierarchy of the Roman Catholic Church that a literary or similar work is free from error in matters of Roman Catholic doctrine and morals, and hence acceptable reading for faithful Catholics.
14 *America*, October 15, 1966.

Chapter Nine
"They'll Know We Are Christians"

We are one in the Spirit, we are one in the Lord.
We are one in the Spirit, we are one in the Lord.
And we pray that all unity may one day be restored.

And they'll know we are Christians by our love, by our love.
Yes, they'll know we are Christians by our love.[1]

—Peter Scholtes

Mass for Young Americans clearly resonated with liturgical America, and pastoral musicians everywhere clamored for more. That demand was more than adequately met by *Hymnal for Young Christians,* which helped to generate an explosion of Folk Mass artists in 1967.

Although it did not and could not include every composer, the best-selling hymnal was tangible proof that the Folk Mass was here to stay. Dennis Fitzpatrick was now busy with the details of running his growing company, but he continued to make decisions on the music and had hands-on involvement with a song that would become the signature work of both FEL and the entire Folk Mass movement.

Peter Scholtes

"They'll Know We Are Christians" was composed by Father Peter Scholtes (b. 1938), associate pastor at Saint Brendan Parish in Chicago's South Side. He was actively involved in the ecumenical movement and was thrilled to host Dr. Martin Luther King, Jr., as a speaker at the church. A guitar-playing folk musician blessed with a delightful voice, Father Scholtes was highly concerned with the gangs of idle youth that beset the community. Realizing that music was a way to attract young people into the life of the parish, he eventually formed them into the St. Brendan's Choir and composed a Mass setting for them with the ear-catching name *Missa Bossa Nova.* Its simple two-chord structure enabled just about any kid in the neighborhood to participate, and they came in droves, bringing bongos, guitars, maracas, and, according to legend, knives — played as percussion! But it was the priest's minor-key anthem to Christian unity that really got Fitzpatrick's attention.

"I immediately knew that 'They'll Know We Are Christians' was special," Fitzpatrick recalls. "By this time I was getting into folk music. My ear was better and my taste was developing. I had started to record some non-liturgical folk artists, like Win Stracke [d. 1991] and Ray Tate. So, yes, I knew when I heard 'Christians' that it was really good."[2] Fitzpatrick even went so far as to personally arrange the choral harmony for this song, a service he did not perform for any other FEL artist.

Although banned in some dioceses, including the Archdiocese of Dallas, *Missa Bossa Nova* became one of the most popular Mass settings of the 1960s. Above all, Scholtes was proud of the involvement of his young people in the life of their parish.

> This group of 40 ghetto youngsters, some of them gang members, really take a lot of pride in their choir. They come from 15 different schools on the South Side of Chicago. Their neighborhood is a ghetto, though not as bad as some. Still, there are lots of gangs, violence, crime, broken homes, congestion, and poverty. There isn't much going for these kids except the choir!
>
> Fr. Scholtes and the choir have been enthusiastically received throughout the country on their concert tours. He is active in ecumenical affairs nationally, and is in great demand as a lecturer. Fans of his music have acclaimed him "a contemporary prophet."[3]

Peter Scholtes' landmark song went on to become a classic, well-loved by Christians of all denominations. Although criticized as overly simplistic, this comes from the heart of its message, taken from John 13:35: "This is how all will know that you are my disciples: your love for one another." Also known by its first line, "We are one in the Spirit," the song became an anthem for the Jesus movement of the early 1970s and is still occasionally recorded by contemporary Christian artists like Jars of Clay, whose 2005 alternative rock rendition helped revive the song's popularity with a new generation.

Scholtes eventually left the priesthood, married, and carved out a new career as an author, lecturer, and consultant in the field of corporate quality management. He is the author of *The Leaders Handbook: Making Things Happen and Getting Things Done*. Recently retired, Peter Scholtes is involved in occasional consulting work and still speaks proudly and fondly of "They'll Know We Are Christians" and its legacy in Christian music.

Paul Quinlan

Born in 1939 into a family of folk singers at Natick, Massachusetts, Paul Quinlan graduated from Dartmouth College in 1960 and joined the Jesuit community as a seminarian at Weston College. In 1965, the America Record Society released *Glory Bound: Psalms Set to Folk Music*. Distributed by World Library of Sacred Music, this was Paul's debut LP and is considered the first recording of religious folk music by a Catholic artist.

Glory Bound, featuring a Roman-collared Quinlan on the cover clutching his guitar, was critically praised and is fondly remembered by the singer's fans. Paul's soft, expressive tenor was backed only with his classically played guitar. The fifteen tracks were musical settings of the Psalms, which would be Quinlan's consistent source of inspiration throughout his composing career.

In the fall of 1965, Quinlan joined the faculty at College of the Holy Cross in Worcester, Massachusetts, to teach philosophy as a "scholastic," the designation for young Jesuits teaching under temporary vows. A daily Folk Mass had begun at Holy Cross under the leadership of Rich Regan, a sophomore guitarist, and Quinlan soon found an outlet for singing his "folk Psalms." Paul and Rich hit it off from the start, and Rich was more than happy to learn his new friend's growing repertoire of original songs.

"We were getting a sizeable core group of daily Mass attendees," Regan remembered. "Most of them were students at the college, and they loved Paul's music as I did. We all knew we had something very special and really looked forward to attending the Mass every day."[4]

The Holy Cross Folk Mass grew in popularity and was noted in the college newspaper: "Attendance at daily Mass jumped to 300. When folk music was added to the Saturday Midnight Mass, two-thirds of the students became regulars."[5]

Quinlan and Regan harmonized well as a duo. Steve Seery, an ROTC student, attended the daily liturgy and soon offered his services as a singer. Regan said this was the start of the Paul Quinlan Trio. "Steve had been a member of a choir somewhere and he had an excellent ear for hearing a third part of a song. His gifts and personality and spirituality made him the perfect complement and balance to Paul and me."[6]

Word of the Holy Cross Folk Masses spread beyond campus and soon the Paul Quinlan Trio was deluged with requests for concert appearances all over the East Coast, performing at Catholic colleges and ecumenical gatherings. Their most memorable concert was on February 7, 1967, at Carnegie Hall. Regan explained how this came about.

"This gig was the result of Jesuit music critic C.J. McNaspy [1915–1995], pulling together six different singers or groups to form a concert held at Carnegie Hall which he named, after a Quinlan song of the same title, 'Praise the Lord in Many Voices.' The idea of the concert was to introduce to the public the new musical innovations going on in the Church at the time."[7]

At this concert, the Trio sang several songs from their standard repertoire, along with two new compositions that would become Quinlan's most popular songs: "Sing to God a Brand New Canticle" and "It's a Brand New Day."

Both songs showcased Paul's penchant for utilizing long verses and equally long refrains. Yet, because of the sheer catchiness of the melodies, congregations easily seized upon them and wouldn't let them go. The former, a minor key favorite with jazzy syncopation, was a spirited rendition of Psalm 98. The latter, with a guitar-strummed hook reminiscent of Peter, Paul & Mary's arrangement of "If I Had My Way" (by Rev. Gary Davis, 1896–1972), was the epitome of 1960s optimism. A free adaptation of Psalm 19, the lyrics of "It's a Brand New Day" seemed to inspire all who sang along to reach out to a world filled with endless possibility:

> It's a brand new day. Everything is fine.
> 'Though it may be gray, I want you to know that the sun's gonna shine.
> And out of that sky, piercing every cloud is our God on high!
>
> There will be a new heart for every man,
> like the flowers that come in early spring.
> For every life there is a plan, no matter what autumn breezes bring.
>
> So put away care, let freedom be yours.
> Joy is everywhere! Joy is everywhere!
> Let freedom ring, alleluia now! Everybody sing!
> Let our voices shout to a mighty king.
>
> © 1975, 1980 by North American Liturgy Resources. (Now owned and administered by OCP.)

Indeed, if the church hymn board posted the number for this song as the recessional, Folk Mass congregations couldn't wait for the priest's final blessing so they could sing it. The songs of Paul Quinlan had that sing-along quality that reflected popular folk music at its best.

The Carnegie Hall concert was released as a three-record set, with the Paul Quinlan Trio performance as Volume 2. The three friends went on to record the *Run Like a Deer* LP for FEL Publications with most of those tracks published in the *Hymnal for Young Christians*. This was the last recorded work of the Paul Quinlan Trio as the student members graduated from Holy Cross soon thereafter.

As a Jesuit, Quinlan tried his best to balance his growing music career with his community commitments. Eventually, he moved on from the order and, during the early 1970s, took up a staff position in Phoenix at North American Liturgy Resources, the new publisher of Folk Mass music started by Ray Bruno, formerly of World Library of Sacred Music. A few years later, he dropped out of involvement with the Church altogether, moving back to Boston with his wife, Nancy.

For a generation of American Catholics, the upbeat songs of Paul Quinlan will always have a treasured place in their hearts. The composer's Folk Mass legacy is perhaps best expressed by the man himself in a 1967 interview.

> Folk singing and the Folk Mass involve everyone in the church. No one is locked up inside his own shell, silently praying. There are times we all need silence and aloneness with God, but in a world of great loneliness and even greater barriers between people, the Church must be a meeting ground, providing a sense of brotherhood through sharing.
>
> The Mass can adapt to many forms of music, but the Folk Mass and folk music is easier to sing, is an integral part of the American culture, and is joyous.[8]

Sister Germaine Habjan

The guitar was a "going away" gift for a talented young woman who seemed to have everything going for her: beauty, personality, and an abundance of musical gifts. Germaine Habjan (b. 1944) sang in the glee club, starred in her high school musicals, and was popular among her classmates. But soon after graduation she joined the Glenmary Home Mission Sisters to serve the poor in rural and small-town America. It was 1961 and the new decade was bright with promise and idealism.

Germaine's parents, Mr. and Mrs. Valentine Habjan of Euclid, Ohio, were Slovanian immigrants who instilled in their children a love for music. "Harmonizing and singing while my father played violin and my mother piano were just part of my daily life," Germaine recalled. "I learned to play [my guitar] and in 1962, when I was working in Appalachia, I became interested in Negro spirituals. They seemed to express human faith so beautifully. After that I started making up my own songs, composing lyrics and tunes suitable to my own experiences."[9]

Sister Germaine entered Marquette University in Milwaukee, Wisconsin, majoring in Communication Arts, but her studies were sidetracked when she began performing her songs at campus and parish events and with interfaith groups. Word got out about this "Singing Nun" and that led to a feature article in the *Saturday Evening Post*.

> Even the student sisters of the Glenmarys are different. Eight of them live in a house in Milwaukee, where they are studying for degrees in history, sociology, English, fine arts, and other fields. Sister Germaine Habjan composes folk songs, which the entire community sings. Last November, two graduate students from Marquette were married, and the whole group sang two of Sister Germaine's songs: "Love One Another" and "All of My Life, I Will Sing Praise to My God."[10]

As mentioned in chapter 7, Milwaukee's Archbishop Cousins banned the use of folk music at liturgy in his archdiocese, but that did not hinder Sister Germaine from her newfound music ministry, which expanded nationally after FEL Publications discovered her. The company rush-released the young nun's *Songs of Salvation* in time for the 1966 Houston Liturgical Week conference, where she created a sensation by performing in her religious habit. FEL's Thomas Cook remembered the shock and delight that met this artist when she performed on the road.

"We had what was considered by many people a very scandalous thing at the time: Sister Germaine, the Glenmary sister. We sent her out to San Francisco and she played in the coffee houses, habit and all. A lot of people thought that was the most scandalous thing that could have happened to the Church. A nun playing in a coffee house!"[11]

Sister Germaine was simply being true to her ministry to bring Christ to the world, whether it was in the rural Appalachians or the Hungry I nightclub. "My songs are about Christians who are involved and in step with the times, not removed from the realities of today," she said. "Some of the songs are ballads, love songs, pieces about friendship and fidelity. Some ask questions. I have my own compositions to choose from, but many times I combine my songs with other folk favorites."[12] True to her questioning generation, Germaine often stirred things up in her concerts.

> Sister Germaine, dressed in the light grey jacket and skirt of her order, captivated the vast audience with her whistling, melodious singing, and fine guitar manipulation. The pink-lighted Imperial Ballroom radiated with flashes of emotions — sorrow, joy, laughter, sadness, hope, trust and love, as she poured forth her songs. When introducing a song about the prodigal son, Sister Germaine told the assembly that "you must become rebellious, ahem!" and the young crowd seethed with the rebelliousness characteristic of so much of the restless younger members of the Church....[13]

Songs of Salvation also became a catechetical resource that was popular in religious education classrooms. With songs based entirely on Scripture, the composer introduced each track with commentary that assisted her young listeners and their teachers to break open God's word.

But the decade's "sacred vs. secular" tug-of-war took its toll on the nation's religious, and Sister Germaine was no exception. She moved on from her community in 1967 to take up a career in teaching that began with an assistantship in speech and drama at Marquette University. She eventually married and left her music career behind. But her signature song, "Love One Another," continues to be sung and was, in fact, performed at the wedding of her daughter Lisa in 2007. The song stands as an apt testimony to an enthusiastic spirit who briefly set the Catholic world on fire when the Folk Mass was in vogue.

> Love one another, love one another as I have loved you.
> And care for each other, care for each other, as I have cared for you.
>
> And bear one another's burdens, and share each other's joys.
> And love one another, love one another, and bring each other home.
> © 1966, FEL Publications. Assigned to Lorenz Corporation.

·■·

There were several other popular composers in *Hymnal for Young Christians* (HYC). Father Ian Mitchell, an Episcopalian priest, had eight songs in *HYC* and would go on to produce *Songs of Protest and Love,* a spirited collaboration with his wife Carolyn that blended sacred and secular folk music. Fr. Mitchell also composed *The American Folk-Song Mass* and *The Jazz-Rock Mass,* which FEL made available in both Anglican and Roman Catholic texts. Mitchell's most popular songs included "Kill I Never Will" and an adaptation of "There's a Wideness in God's Mercy."

Robert Blue was a student at Eden Seminary, a St. Louis inter-denominational school for ordained and lay ministry. Blue was very successful in composing music specifically for children, and many Sunday School and CCD children enjoyed singing his songs "Run, Come See" and "The Witness Song." He also composed a popular setting of the Magnificat, as well as the haunting "Give Me Your Hand."

Hymnal for Young Christians also included music by composers not under exclusive contract with FEL, giving wider exposure to Father Clarence Rivers' "God Is Love," "God the Father," and "Bless the Lord." At this time, Fr. Rivers released his ambitious World Library LP album, *A Mass Dedicated to the Brotherhood of Man*, a critically acclaimed Mass setting that featured a jazz combo, a parish choir, and the Cincinnati Symphony Orchestra.

The songs of Father Willard Jabusch (b. 1930) became very popular because of *Hymnal for Young Christians*. A priest and seminary professor of the Archdiocese of Chicago, Fr. Jabusch specialized in adapting the folk tunes of other nations and writing new English liturgical lyrics for them. The most famous of these are "The King of Glory" and "Song of Good News," both based on Israeli folk melodies. Fr. Jabusch also penned the popular social justice hymn, "Whatsoever You Do" (with text inspired by Matthew 25:35–46).

Hymnal for Young Christians could not, of course, feature every Folk Mass composer. Among those not included are two of the most noteworthy Catholic artists of their times.

Joe Wise

An acknowledged pioneer of the Folk Mass movement, Joe Wise (b. 1939) was a seminarian when the Second Vatican Council was in session, attending Saint Mary's Seminary in Baltimore, Maryland, the same school that would later produce Folk Mass composers Jack Miffleton (b. 1942), Tom Parker, Neil Blunt, and C.P. Mudd (1944–2005). Wise shared the idealism and promise of the early 1960s with his fellow seminarians, as well as a love for folk music, and he found in the Folk Mass a way to bring all those elements together.

Although he left Saint Mary's, Wise continued to lead worship at local parishes while running a coffee shop. It was 1966, the year Paul Quinlan, Ray Repp, and others were experimenting with folk music at their community liturgies. During a liturgical gathering in Memphis, Wise had a life-changing encounter with Father Clarence Rivers.

"He was in Memphis, and he heard my music, and he gave me three thousand dollars of his own money," Wise remembered. "He said, 'If you don't sell enough to pay me back, fine. If you do earn the money, pay me back without interest.' It was an awesome gift."[14] Wise made a monaural tape, started his own publishing company, Fontaine House, and arranged to have his new LP record distributed by Rivers' publisher, World Library of Sacred Music.

Released in the Fall of 1966, *Gonna Sing My Lord* is considered a landmark Folk Mass album. Simply recorded, with the classic string band accompaniment of guitars, banjo, and upright bass, Wise's debut collection had the stark live-performance feel that characterized the early Folk Mass records. It had songs for the various ritual parts of the Mass, including a musical setting of an anamnesis acclamation (anticipating by four years the Roman rite's adoption of the memorial acclamation). But it was Joe's original lyrics and melodies that left the deepest impression on the fledgling Folk Mass repertoire.

The album's title song was a plaintive litany of hope in which the singer promises to give his whole self to God "till I see your face." "Sing Praise to the Lord" was a personal cry that reflected the younger generation's search for self, within a Christian context:

> He tells me joy is dying with him, nailed is to be free.
> His weary arms reach out for my love.
> When will I ever be me? When will I ever be me?
> © 1966 by World Library Publications, Inc.

Good as these were, it was in "Take Our Bread" that Wise found his signature song. Modestly subtitled "An Offertory Hymn" and sung on the record with heartfelt vocals and a solo guitar, this song quickly became a popular favorite of many Folk Mass congregations. The lyrics tapped into the then-current trend of personalizing the rites of the liturgy in a way that showcased a familiar, almost casual relationship with the Almighty.

> Take our bread, we ask you. Take our hearts, we love you.
> Take our lives, oh Father, we are yours, we are yours.
>
> Yours as we stand at the table you set.
> Yours as we eat the bread our hearts can't forget.
> We are the sign of your life with us yet.
> We are yours, we are yours.
>
> Your holy people standing washed in your blood;
> Spirit-filled yet hungry, we await your food.
> We are poor but we've brought ourselves the best we could.
> We are yours, we are yours.
> ©1966 by World Library Publications, Inc.

Gonna Sing My Lord was an immediate hit. Wise quit his coffee shop job and began a lifelong career of touring and singing at concerts, conferences, workshops, and liturgies throughout the English-speaking world. Bruce Bruno remembers helping his father Ray in supporting the singer's events for World Library.

> "Joe had such a simple performance. He would sit on a stool on stage with his guitar, and a microphone in front of him. That was it. I can still picture him. He was just there, engaging the people with his stories and his songs."[15]

Wise's Folk Mass peers have fond memories of him. "Joe was an excellent singer," Jack Miffleton recalled. "He could entertain, and he could put across things, and he was a great retreat leader. He just had a way with young people because he could sing so well."[16]

"Joe Wise was with us at one of the first appearances of the Dameans, at the CYO [Catholic Youth Organization] convention in Baton Rouge," said Gary Ault. "I was thrilled because 'Take Our Bread' was a standard in our liturgies. We sang with him and I remember doing 'Four Strong Winds' and 'There's a Meeting Here Tonight.'"[17]

Somehow, in the midst of his busy schedule, Wise managed to earn four degrees in philosophy; theology; education; and counseling and guidance. He eventually recorded 22 albums, with many collections of music for children in collaboration with his wife, Maleita. Wise has published three books, scored a film, and wrote an article for *Sports Illustrated*.[18] He studied art, specializing in watercolors, and his award-winning paintings hang in corporate headquarters and private collections across the United States.

Always a searcher, Wise now embraces a non-denominational spiritual path. But he remembers where he came from and is grateful. In the liner notes of his 1994 retrospective CD, *Most Requested: Music for the Spirit,* Wise wrote:

> Thanks to all of you who supported my work and music for so many years. My life energies and spiritual path find me no longer in many of your arenas, but I am grateful for the rich and abundant opportunities you gave me for so long.
>
> The Lord lets His face shine down upon you,
> The sun rises up to meet you on your way,
> The Spirit of Her (*sic*) love invades the circle of your friends,
> Your vision keeps you changing day by day.[19]

Joe and Maleita Wise currently reside in Arizona and are actively involved in giving workshops and retreats in art, journaling, writing, and meditation.

Sebastian Temple

Johann Sebastian Templehoff (1928–1997), better known as Sebastian Temple, was a son of the South African veldt, born in Pretoria. When he was three years old, his Jewish mother died giving birth to her second child, and his paternal grandparents raised him as a fundamentalist Christian. Thus began a lifelong search in which young Sebastian tried many paths to God.

At 16, he wrote a romantic novel in his native Afrikaans, *Die Hel se SpeelgrOnde,* and the royalties enabled him to travel to Italy, where he studied anthropology and pre-Renaissance art. Temple moved to London in 1951 and worked for the BBC as a news broadcaster. After several years he went to India to live as a monk in a Hindu monastery, and in 1958 he arrived in America, where he joined the Church of Scientology. He dropped out of that organization and converted to Catholicism. Temple was unsuccessful in his efforts to become a priest, but he joined the Franciscan secular

Third Order and adopted their simple lifestyle, settling in Los Angeles.

Around this time, Temple became interested in exploring his mother's Jewish roots and he wanted to compose music with a Jewish writer. By chance, he found Sarah Hershberg, an up-and-coming folk singer and songwriter.

"Working with Sebastian was truly an eye-opener," Hershberg remembered. "I was brought up in a secular home. We were very Jewish and very nationalistic, but not religious. Sebastian was the first God-intoxicated person I had ever met in my life. He brought God and religion into my life, something totally new and unusual.

"He explored so many different spiritual avenues, all leading to the same end, which was, for him, having a personal experience with God, what he called 'knowing God.' He went through all kinds of disciplines to reach that goal."[20]

So great was their rapport that the two composers produced many noteworthy albums: *Great Day in Bethlehem*; *Moses in Story and Song*; *Good, Good*; and *Genesis Too*, their ecumenical collaboration very much in keeping with the spirit of Vatican II. In 1965, Temple also released a collection of secular folk music on Capitol Records, *Africa Belongs to the Lion*, which showcased his homeland roots as a composer.

Given Temple's convert zeal and his talents as a folk singer, it wasn't long before he turned his attention to composing music for the burgeoning Folk Mass. St. Francis Productions, the communications arm of the Franciscan community in Los Angeles, approached Temple about producing a collection of songs centered on the life and spirituality of their founder. Entitled *Happy the Man,* this album is most notable as the first vehicle for one of the most enduring songs of the Folk Mass era, "Make Me a Channel of Your Peace." The composer vividly remembered the day he wrote it.

> I wrote so easily and so prolifically that I took for granted that I could write music to the peace prayer of Saint Francis. The album's other twelve songs fell out of my lips and onto a tape recorder very easily and I wrote them in two days. The third day was left for the peace prayer. Though inspirations for all came easily to me, its strange form drove me crazy. I could not come up with anything that sounded like music to my ears. I tried for a whole morning but nothing came. Finally, I was disgusted, looked at the little statue of Saint Francis on my shelf and said angrily, "Well, if you want to write it, YOU do it. I can't." I got up, went to the kitchen, made a cup of tea and drank it. When I returned to the guitar, I picked it up, had the tape running, and the song fell out of my mouth as it was recorded a few days later.[21]

Temple's later compositions became a body of work that was especially popular with Folk Mass enthusiasts. "The Living God," "Sing! People of God, Sing," "All That I Am," "Prayer for Peace," "We Are One," and "Take My Hands" seemed to stand out from the songs of his Folk Mass peers. Perhaps it was because Temple's song form and chord choices owed more to the German/Dutch/South African style of folk music, in contrast with the American folk music tradition of Ray Repp, Paul Quinlan, and Joe Wise. Temple's approach was more simple and direct, and that was certainly born out in his most famous song.

> Make me a channel of your peace.
> Where there is hatred, let me bring your love.
> Where there is injury your pardon, Lord,
> And where there's doubt, true faith in you.
>
> Make me a channel of your peace.
> Where there's despair in life, let me bring hope.
> Where there is darkness, only light, And where there's sadness, ever joy.
>
> Oh, Master, grant that I may never seek
> So much to be consoled as to console,
> To be understood as to understand,
> To be loved as to love with all my soul.
>
> Make me a channel of your peace.
> It is in pardoning that we are pardoned,
> In giving to all [men] that we receive,
> And in dying that we're born to eternal life.
>
> © 1967, 2003, OCP Publications. Dedicated to Mrs. Frances Tracy.

"He took everything in stride when it came to his songs," Hershberg observed. "The truth is he never really took full credit. He always said, 'God is working through me.'"[22]

Temple became fascinated with the writings of the then-controversial Jesuit Father Pierre Teilhard de Chardin (1881–1955) and in 1970 released *The Universe Is Singing*, a collection of folk music that condensed and expressed the heady ideas of the theologian for a mass audience. For a short while, he went on the lecture circuit to promote Teilhard, and then abruptly dropped out of music altogether, preferring to express his spiritual journey in a series of poems that eventually became published in his 1995 book, *Running Free*. Raw in its honesty and beauty, these poems offer an intimate glimpse of a man who had spent his whole life searching for God.

> After daily being "in heaven," slowly the consolations began to withdraw and I drifted into the dark night — for me a terrible depression that ravaged me so completely that at times I thought that I would die, or worse, that I wouldn't die — or just go completely insane. Psychologists call this a clinical depression, and it had all the symptoms, but I saw priests who knew the signs and symptoms of this state. They said it was the dark night....[23]

Temple had moved to Tucson, Arizona, and continued to live the simple Franciscan lifestyle. Although he struggled financially, the artist became involved with charitable works. He started a foundation to deliver clothes, supplies, and money to the poor in Mexico. Sebastian Temple seemed content to live the rest of his days in relative obscurity, serving the poor. And then, events halfway around the world transformed his life.

On August 31, 1997, Princess Diana of Wales was killed in a car accident that shocked the world. An estimated global audience of 2.5 billion people watched the televised funeral at Westminster Abbey. The service was a unique blend of contemporary and traditional music, and the emotional high point for many was Elton John's new rendition of his song "Candle in the Wind," which he sang as a tribute for Diana entitled "Goodbye, England's Rose." Many people, including Diana's son Harry, were brought to tears. The Westminster Boys Choir followed with a lovely arrangement of a song that immediately lifted the world's spirits after the rock star's performance.

"Make me a channel of your peace . . ."

Sarah Hershberg would always remember that moment. "I stayed up until 3:00 in the morning because I wanted to watch the funeral. All of a sudden, I heard the song and I couldn't believe it. I waited until 7:00 AM to call Sebastian in Tucson to tell him I heard it, and I hoped I wasn't waking him. And he said, 'Oh, Sarah! You didn't awaken me. People have been calling me from all over the world!' Everybody knew the song and everybody was amazed to hear it at the funeral. The Westminster choirmaster called him for permission. Sebastian said yes, but he didn't call any of his friends to tell them to listen. I'm not sure he actually believed it was going to be done and it was as much a shock to him as it was to the rest of us."[24]

This highly visible exposure led to a resurgence of interest in Temple's music. More artists recorded "Make Me a Channel," including Sinead O'Connor, and choirs everywhere wanted to sing it, prompting a new sheet music release by OCP, who now owns and administers the copyright. A very substantial royalty check was sent to the composer, the largest he had ever received. Sadly, Temple died soon after from a heart attack.

Over the years, there have been many renditions of the Prayer of Saint Francis, but Temple's version endures because he truly captured the simplicity of Saint Francis himself. The song was a favorite of Princess Diana and, through her, it touched the world. Before his death, the composer sent this letter to Martin Neary, organist and master of choristers at Westminster Abbey.

> Dear Mr. Neary:
>
> It is with great pleasure that I am writing you this letter, long overdue. When I heard your arrangement of "Make me a Channel of Your Peace" at the funeral of Princess Diana I cried.
>
> Thank you. It has always pained me that I couldn't read or write music, but each time I tried, something came up to stop me until I thought that

perhaps the Lord did not want me to be so musically educated. The truth is that I didn't even like the song when it flowed through me. But to hear what you did to it delighted me so that I changed my mind and now I am happy to have been the instrument of God's peace in the composition of that song.

You made it sound so right and so perfect. How can I not be grateful to you for the privilege of hearing it as it should sound?

I must also admit that the whole funeral service was totally unforgettable. All the music thrilled. Princess Diana's death certainly stirred a universal archetype deep within us all.

Thank you for affecting me as you did. May you be blessed forever.

Gratefully your friend and admirer,

—Sebastian Temple[25]

· ■ ·

The Folk Mass composers were the troubadours of their generation, asking their questions and searching for answers in the God of their everyday experience. American Catholics would need this optimism as the decade embarked upon its most tumultuous year.

---

1 "They'll Know We Are Christians" © 1966, FEL Church Publications, Ltd., assigned 1991 to Lorenz Publishing Company.
2 Interview with the author, May 15 and 16, 2007, Las Vegas, Nevada.
3 FEL news release, 1968.
4 Interview with the author, Spring 2008.
5 *Holy Cross College Newspaper*. The Saturday Midnight Mass was initially discussed in chapter 7.
6 Interview with the author, Spring 2008.
7 Interview with the author, Spring 2008.
8 *Pictorial Living Coloroto Magazine*, a Sunday section of the *New York Daily News*, January 22, 1967.
9 Gassaway, Melinda, "She Tells His Story by Singing," *Daily Breeze* (Los Angeles), Wednesday, July 12, 1967.
10 "The New Nuns," *Saturday Evening Post*, July 30, 1966.
11 Interview with the author, December 28, 2003, Los Angeles, California.
12 Gassaway, Melinda, "She Tells His Story by Singing," *Daily Breeze* (Los Angeles), Wednesday, July 12, 1967.
13 From an unattributed press release printed in the liner notes of *The Best of Ray Repp, Vol. 1*, a 2004 CD retrospective of the early works of Ray Repp.
14 McDannell, Colleen, *Religions of the United States in Practice* (Princeton University Press: 2001) 105.
15 Interview with the author, February 10, 2007, Beaverton, Oregon.
16 Interview with the author, March 8, 2007, Martinez, California.
17 Interview with the author, January 6, 2006, New Orleans, Louisiana.
18 "Aching for Basketball," *Sports Illustrated*, December 18, 1989. This was Joe Wise's whimsical reflection on basketball leagues for middle-aged men.
19 Liner notes from the CD *Most Requested: Music for the Spirit* by Joe Wise, ©1994 by GIA Publications, Inc.

20 Interview with the author, May 2, 2008, by phone from Encino, California. Sarah Hershberg was a pioneer in contemporary Jewish liturgy as the first woman to write, compose, and present a Friday evening Sabbath service. She composed a solo collection with FEL Publications entitled *Women of the Old Testament,* with many songs that were included in *Hymnal for Young Christians, Volume 2.*
21 Bradley, Ian, *The Book of Hymns* (New York: Random House / Testament Books, 1989) 264–265.
22 Interview with the author, May 2, 2008, by phone from Encino, California.
23 Temple, Sebastian, *Running Free* (Long Beach, CA: Wenzel Press, 1995) 8.
24 Interview with the author, May 2, 2008, by phone from Encino, California.
25 Letter dated October 17, 1997. As quoted in the *Catholic Sentinel* (Archdiocese of Portland in Oregon), Vol. 128, Number 51, December 19, 1997.

Chapter Ten
"We Shall Overcome"

> The year 1968 was a terrible year and yet one for which many people feel nostalgia. Despite the thousands dead in Vietnam, the million starved in Biafra, the crushing of idealism in Poland and Czechoslovakia, the massacre in Mexico, the clubbings and brutalization of dissenters all over the world, the murder of two Americans who most offered the world hope, to many it was a year of great possibilities....[1]
>
> —Mark Kurlansky, *1968: The Year That Rocked the World*

In a decade already on overload, 1968 went over the top. This was the year when the issues, ideals, and frustrations of the entire decade exploded into *Gotterdammerung*. Nothing was safe from 1968's unrelenting wave of confrontation and change.

The decade that started out with such bright promise was marching steadily into darkness, and the road was marked with a murdered President, an escalating and unpopular war, racial conflict, urban unrest, college campus demonstrations, and a challenged morality. America needed light.

As the year began, two beacons of hope were shining brightly. Martin Luther King, Jr. (1929–1968) still had a dream that "we will be able to transform the jangling discords of our nation into a beautiful symphony of brotherhood."[2]

Senator Robert F. Kennedy (1925–1968), still hurting from his brother's assassination, had his own dream to fulfill: to help make America great by inspiring its people, especially its young people, to look honestly and compassionately at the problems of the day and work together to build the future.

One of these lights was extinguished on April 4, when King was brutally gunned down while laboring in support of better working conditions for the sanitation workers of Memphis, Tennessee. On June 5, the other light died when Kennedy was shot in Los Angeles on the night of a victorious California primary election that solidified his position as the Democratic Party's candidate for President. With sad irony, his last words, spoken from the podium to his exuberant supporters, were: "I think we can end the divisions within America...the violence."[3]

The twin assassinations sapped the nation's spirit, and the despair was palpable and disconcerting. Even so, American Catholics continued to sing of their optimism at liturgy as they celebrated the Second Vatican Council's call to establish "a kingdom of justice, love and peace."[4] Was this hopeful spirit hollow and naïve? Rooted in the enthusiasm of the early 1960s and personified by President Kennedy and

Pope John XXIII, the Folk Mass helped young Catholics make sense of a world that was tumbling out of control.

1968 saw the debut of four major new Folk Mass artists.

John Fischer

John Fischer (b. 1947) joined Robert Blue as the only Folk Mass composers to come from a non-liturgical tradition.[5] Growing up in Pasadena, California, Fischer's involvement in the Congregational Church grounded him in Baptist theology.

"1968 was when I first started writing. I loved folk music, and I found folk and folk-rock to be a very passionate force in our culture for things beyond just falling in love. There are lots of messages involved: civil rights, the war in Vietnam, and peace, and love, making a new world, and all those things. Well, if we're going to have all that, why not have a spiritual preaching message? Why not have a message of faith? And once that barrier was removed between my spirituality and music, then it was a simple step to start writing."[6]

Fischer started singing his songs at Wheaton College in Illinois and at a Christian summer camp at Mt. Hermon, California. He pitched his music to some Protestant record labels but they never responded. "They were not that daring back then," Fischer recalls, "not quite ready yet for rock-based Christian music. The Catholic Church was actually ahead in this, with the Folk Mass." His work at Mt. Hermon caught the attention of FEL's Jim Schaefer, who contacted the singer and requested a demo tape, commencing a collaboration that resulted in two landmark albums: *The Cold Cathedral* and *Have You Seen Jesus, My Lord*.

Fischer's albums raised the bar in FEL's production values. As late as 1967, FEL's albums still sounded like demonstration records. *The Cold Cathedral* and *Jesus, My Lord* were fully realized with an outright folk-rock sound. They were meant to be listened to, not just to teach the Folk Mass choir a new song. The artist's songwriting, arranging, and vocal performance were radio-ready and, in fact, Fischer is often referred to as "the undisputed senior statesman of Contemporary Christian Music."[7] *The Cold Cathedral* was released several months before Larry Norman's *Upon This Rock*, which is regarded by many observers as the first true record of the Protestant Contemporary Christian Music movement.

"The irony is that even though my album came out before Norman's, nobody in my Protestant circles heard about it because FEL did not have distribution in the Protestant market," Fischer says. He didn't really have much exposure in Catholic circles, either. Although he appeared with other FEL artists at Liturgical Week conferences, the company did not promote him as heavily as Ray Repp or the Dameans. Nevertheless, Fischer's music became popular. "Trust and Obey" was a parish favorite, and "Road of Life" was sung at many high school baccalaureate liturgies. "Jesus, My Lord" became an anthem for the ecumenical Cursillo movement and thousands of participants fondly recall singing the gospel-flavored tune during their retreat weekend.

> Have you seen Jesus, my Lord? He's here in plain view.
> Take a look, open your eyes. He'll show it to you.
>
> Have you ever looked at the cross, with a man hangin' in pain,
> And the look of love in his eyes? Then I say: You've seen Jesus, my Lord.
> © 1970 by Songs and Creations, Inc.

John Fischer went on to bigger fame in Contemporary Christian Music (CCM) after he left FEL and joined the Light label. His most popular CCM songs include "All Day Song (Love Him in the Morning)"; a rendition of "Lord of the Dance"; and the critically acclaimed "Dark Horse." But both Protestant and Catholic audiences still rise to their feet whenever he performs "Jesus, My Lord." He continues to compose music and has also made a name for himself as a Christian writer, lecturer, radio personality, and columnist for *CCM* magazine. John Fischer is the undeniable bridge between the Catholic Folk Mass movement and the Protestant CCM movement.

Carey Landry

"Carey and Gary" sang their favorite folk songs in 1966 on talent night at Notre Dame Seminary in New Orleans, and that meant Peter, Paul & Mary; the Kingston Trio; and the calypso hits of Harry Belafonte. Carey sang lead and Gary harmonized while playing guitar. It was all fun and innocent, born of the need for informal community entertainment at a post-Conciliar seminary. No one in that audience could predict that these two would go on to become giants in the liturgical field: Gary Ault as co-founder of the Dameans, and Carey Landry as co-creator of the enormously successful *Hi, God* series of catechetical music for children.

But Notre Dame was not yet celebrating Folk Masses. Steeped in chant and choral music, Landry attended a liturgical conference in Texas where he observed Joe Wise in action.

"I just kind of stood in the back and watched this Folk Mass going on, not quite believing what I was seeing. It was so foreign to me and I was dumbfounded by it."[8]

The next year, Landry transferred to The Catholic University in Washington, D.C., continuing his studies for the Diocese of Lafayette, Louisiana. It was at the Theological College there that he began to experience the Folk Mass on a weekly basis.

"That's where I became so enamored of it and just enthralled with it," Landry remembers. "By then I had learned to play the guitar a little bit, and then participated in the group, and finally began to lead them."

The weekly Folk Mass at Theological College was open to the general public, and it typically attracted a large crowd of people from around the capital region. Musicians and pastoral teams approached Landry and invited him to visit their parishes and help establish their own folk liturgies. At one point, Landry became involved in five or six parishes a month.

"When I came to Washington there was something called the Action Mass, which was a traveling liturgy that involved folk music. And we would sort of go from one parish to another, whoever would accept us, and do a Folk Mass." The college administration encouraged this ministry as part of their post-Conciliar outreach to the community.

Inspired by Vatican II and the social justice bent of 1960's folk music, Landry's first composition was a song that would become his personal anthem for the Folk Mass movement.

> The Spirit is a-movin' all over, all over this land.
> Old ones are dreaming dreams, And young men and women see the light.
> © 1969, 1979, Carey Landry and OCP.

"The Spirit Is a-Movin'" expressed a much-needed optimism within a liturgical context. Because of the high-profile weekly Folk Masses at Catholic U., augmented by Landry's regional workshops, the song fulfilled its own first line and became popular all over America. This caught the attention of Ray Bruno, who was just beginning to split from the well-established World Library of Sacred Music to form his own company, Epoch-Universal Publications, later known as North American Liturgy Resources (NALR).

Bruce Bruno, son of NALR's publisher, recalls: "World Library received a submission from a young seminarian, and my dad took it to Omer Westendorf and said, 'This stuff is great. We've got to do it.' Omer said, 'No, this will never amount to anything. This guy will never go anywhere.' So that's when my dad left World Library and called Carey and said, 'Omer doesn't want to publish you, but I'll do it, if you'll be brave with me. I'm going start my own company, and I'd love to take you on.'"[9]

The NALR story is a largely 1970s phenomenon that may someday be told. But it is worth noting that the fledgling company struggled with a mix of sacred and secular artists, until they released Landry's groundbreaking collection of music for children, *Hi, God.*

Hi, God probably sold over $1 million worth of products that first year," recalls Landry. "Then other people like the St. Louis Jesuits began to look upon NALR as a viable publishing entity. *Hi, God* literally established NALR."

Hi, God would become the basis of Landry's life work with his friend and future wife, Sister Carol Jean Kinghorn. But that would be in the future. As we shall see, in the late '60s the young composer's work as a regional Folk Mass clinician gave him a fulfilling ministry through which he encountered America's first family of politics.

Jack Miffleton and the Baltimore Seminarians

Only one radio was allowed on campus, and only in the common room to allow the community to hear the evening news. It was 1963, and that was the rule at Saint Mary's Seminary in Baltimore, Maryland. If the seminarians wanted music, they had to make it themselves. And did they ever!

Jack Miffleton was a young saxophonist and piano player with a natural gift for music. The seminarians never bought sheet music because they could always rely on Jack to arrange a song simply by listening to it once on the radio or a record player.

"We had enough guys there to make a big band," Miffleton fondly remembers. "We had three trumpets, a trombone and four saxes, and we played several of the old jazz arrangements of the 1940s and 1950s. The seminary gave us plenty of time to practice. People would sit in their rooms and learn to play the guitar. We would get together and trade licks. Somebody would learn something and teach it to somebody else. We had talent nights that we called '*Gaudeamus*' and we basically were entertaining ourselves."

This fun musical spirit even permeated the traditional seminary wake-up call that, in the early 1960s, consisted of the chanting of "*Benedicamus Domino*" (Let us bless the Lord) throughout the dormitory halls. Seminarians took turns intoning the chant, and the response, in the groans and grunts of a sleeping community, was "*Deo gratias*" (Thanks be to God). One morning, Miffleton's friend Neil Blunt and his roommate Tom Behan decided to sing the wake-up call as an English folk psalm with guitars, long before folk music was allowed at liturgy!

"In 1964, our seminary opened up a bit and allowed us to sing in the neighboring community. We went around to any place that would invite us. We played at various campuses around the area, and we got on local television. Someone would always say, 'Hey, there's a bunch of seminarians that make music!'"[10]

Besides Miffleton, the Baltimore seminarians became a Who's Who list of future Folk Mass composers and artists: Tom Parker, Pat Mudd, Mike Wynn, Phil Esserwein, Skip Sanders, and the aforementioned Neil Blunt.

Miffleton and his fellow seminarians had not set out to become composers, but the confluence of talent was sure to spill over into the liturgy when the Council broke things wide open. Luckily, they had a mentor in Father Jim Burns, Saint Mary's director of music.

"Jim was writing things in English — the introits and other Mass Propers — because the Mass was still partly in Latin and partly in English. He encouraged me and a few others to try our hand at composing. Jim, with his background in music and composition, would challenge us on things that we didn't notice: 'You know, that's a strong accent on that word.' But if you wanted people to sing it, not just as a solo performance, then you had to be attentive to that particular kind of practice. He made us realize that there was much more to composition than meets the eye.

"We quickly started using guitars and piano at liturgy, which was a mixture of different styles of music. We had some chant, and then there would be an offertory song and Communion song done with the guitars, and then a traditional closing hymn. And there would very likely be a Bach postlude, played on the organ. It was all mixed and blended."

Eventually, Father Burns submitted a packet of his students' compositions to World Library. The editors there didn't know what to make of this new music and, after issuing a standard thank you letter, simply put it in their files, where it languished for a few years.

"Then, in 1968, I received a letter from Omer Westendorf saying he had been at a retreat at Grailville near Cincinnati and they were singing this music by Jack Miffleton, scriptural psalms and hymns. 'How can I get ahold of that music?' he said in the letter. And so I wrote him back and said, 'Look in your files. You have what you heard at the retreat.' Omer heard it sung, sang along with it, and then he was interested in putting it together with a professional recording."

That record, *With Skins and Steel,* was released in 1969, shortly after Miffleton's ordination as a priest. A total Saint Mary's production, featuring the voices and instruments of his seminary friends, the album yielded at least one huge liturgical hit, the Easter song "Alle, Alle." Miffleton would go on to release several more albums of Folk Mass music before settling into his life work of composing catechetical music for children. He currently teaches music at Saint Jarlath's School in Oakland, California. He and his wife, Gabriella, own and operate a retirement facility for the elderly where Jack conducts regular sessions in music therapy for the senior residents.

Miffleton's seminary friends also enjoyed success in liturgical music. Tom Parker wrote "Be Consoled," "Lord, Make Us Ready" and other songs that appeared in the collection, *Let All the Earth Sing His Praise,* published by World Library.

C.P. (Pat) Mudd's most popular song was "The Lord Is Risen to Life." Now deceased, he had a distinguished career as a diocesan director of liturgy and has a posthumous CD with OCP.

Neil Blunt produced several collections of music for World Library and NALR, including *No Time Like the Present; Possible Gospel* (with Pat Mudd); and *Come Out!* (children's music with Jack Miffleton). Neil retired as director of the Cincinnati Housing Authority and has a successful second career in real estate, but he has continued working as a musician and music minister.

Mike Wynne had a popular setting of the Magnificat that was published by American Catholic Press. He is the Accounting/CPA advisor for the business school at Baruch College in New York City.

Phil Esserwein is a professional musician and producer working in the Baltimore area. His most popular song was "Abba, Father," published by American Catholic Press.

Although not a composer, Skip Sanders was a gifted vocalist who sang lead on many of the albums produced by the Saint Mary's group. Dr. Sanders is deputy superintendent of Baltimore schools and was recently featured on OCP's gospel album for children, *O Won't You Sit Down,* arranged and produced by Jack Miffleton.

The Dameans

Gary Ault was a high school seminarian with the Maryknoll missionary community when he first heard the music of Father Clarence Rivers. Older seminarians, attending the seminal 1964 St. Louis Liturgical Week, returned with this new music, exposing Gary to a new world of liturgical possibility. He eventually transferred to the minor seminary in Louisiana, where he met Mike Balhoff and Darryl Ducote. Upon graduation, the three friends moved on to Notre Dame Seminary in New Orleans where Ault formed a folk singing duo with Carey Landry.

When Landry relocated to The Catholic University, Ault formed the Notre Dame Seminary Trio with Bob Morgan and Charles Monzelun; they first performed at an ecumenical service singing Joseph Gelineau's "My Shepherd Is the Lord." After Ducote joined the group as a lead singer and Balhoff became their bass player, the group started singing at local parishes to demonstrate the new Folk Mass. Balhoff came up with a catchy group name to honor their school: the Dameans.

Although Morgan and Monzelun eventually left the seminary, Ault didn't have to look too far for replacements. Saint John's Seminary in Little Rock, Arkansas, closed in 1966 and many of its students transferred to Notre Dame, including Dave Baker and Buddy Ceasar. In Arkansas, they had formed their own singing group, the Travelers, entertaining at local coffee houses and nearby college campuses, specializing in the tight vocal harmonies that were the trademark of secular folk groups such as the Kingston Trio. When their seminary closed, Baker and Ceasar wondered if they would be able to continue singing together.

The Arkansas duo was impressed with the group leading the singing at Notre Dame's liturgies. At the same time, the Dameans noticed Baker's and Ceasar's own talents when they sang at a talent show. Ault, Ducote, and Balhoff asked the newcomers to join the Dameans, little realizing that Baker and Ceasar were already conspiring to get themselves invited in.

"Gary and Mike were leading up to asking us to join them," recalls Baker, "and before they really asked, both Buddy and I, with a bit of humor, interrupted them and chimed in 'Yes!' There was a focus and an ease and humor about the way we all related. We easily became friends, as did our families."[11]

Ault remembers, "The first time we met to practice in one of the theology classrooms, I knew there was something there. It was a great sound. We played a CYO convention in Baton Rouge the next weekend and people wanted to know how long we had been playing together — five years? When we told them five days they couldn't believe it."

That first gig in 1968 had its comical moment as the Dameans, formally dressed in their seminary suits and ties, were seen pushing Ducote's car along the side of a road to re-start it. "We sang and sang, all over the country," Ault recalls fondly. "And you haven't seen country until you've been to some of the quaint Louisiana towns of Innis, Darrow, Mix, Cut Off, and many other places off the beaten path." A rather forward-looking seminary faculty approved the Dameans' road ministry as long as they kept up with their studies. Sometimes they were the only ones in the seminary library studying late on a Saturday night.[12]

The changes in the Mass gave the Dameans ample opportunity to write original music, filling the need for fresh liturgical repertoire. Ault and Ducote became the group's most prolific composers, designing their songs to fit in simply within the Mass and the liturgical year: "All That We Have" for the offertory; "Look Beyond" at Communion; "Shout Out Your Joy" for the Easter season. Buddy Ceasar wrote "Service" for a friend's ordination.

Because they were such ardent road warriors, the Dameans eventually caught the attention of FEL Publications. While singing at a conference at Louisiana State University, friends of FEL staffer Thomas Cook were in attendance and immediately called Cook in his Los Angeles office to tell him of the Dameans' great performances. FEL requested a demo that the group recorded in the hallway on the second floor of the seminary building because of its reverberation. Clearly impressed, Jim Schaefer and Roger Nachtwey went to Nashville to record the Dameans' first album, *Tell the World*.

Buddy Ceasar remembers the Nashville sessions as an exciting time. "We did all the playing and singing," Ceasar recalls. "It was simply done, but they also had another person (FEL's Ray Tate) who helped with the arranging and the extra guitar work. *Tell the World* led to more engagements and gave us more confidence. We began writing more, knowing that there was a need. And now we had a big outlet for our creative work. So *Tell the World* really did get us started.

"But soon afterward, Gary, Dave, and I were ordained for three different dioceses. We thought that was going to be the end because the Dameans was more of a seminary experience. And as we received more demands for appearances, we saw that there really was a need for that kind of ministry. We asked our bishops and personnel boards to allow us to use the Dameans as our part-time ministry, and they agreed. We just had to work it out with our pastors, who were very supportive."[13]

Thus began a lifelong ministry and circle of friendship that continues to this day.[14] The Dameans epitomized the Folk Mass movement at its best, and, as we shall see, they would also play a role in helping to reshape composer-publisher relations.

·■·

The Catholic Church was not immune to 1968's relentless march. On June 30, the Sisters of the Immaculate Heart were forced to withdraw from the parish schools where they had taught for decades in the Archdiocese of Los Angeles, their long-standing teaching contracts terminated by James Francis Cardinal McIntyre after years of heated dialog about the order's interpretation of the reforms of Vatican II. One of the sticking points for McIntyre was the order's modernization to secular dress.[15]

On August 10, Father William DuBay, a Los Angeles priest, married Mrs. Mary Ellen Wall, a union that followed several months of activism by DuBay, during which he publicly criticized Cardinal McIntyre for an alleged lack of enthusiasm for racial causes, among other issues.[16]

Both proceedings served as bookends to the summer's main Catholic event. On July 25, as Chicago braced itself for thousands of demonstrators at the Democratic Convention, Pope Paul VI made his long-awaited announcement about a moral subject that personally touched just about everyone in the Church. The announcement was a papal encyclical called *Humanae Vitae*. The topic was artificial birth control. The pope wrote:

> Marriage and conjugal love are by their nature ordained toward the procreation and education of children. Children are really the supreme gift of marriage and contribute in the highest degree to their parents' welfare.
>
> Therefore We base Our words on the first principles of a human and Christian doctrine of marriage when We are obliged once more to declare that the direct interruption of the generative process already begun and, above all, all direct abortion, even for therapeutic reasons, are to be absolutely excluded as lawful means of regulating the number of children. Equally to be condemned, as the magisterium of the Church has affirmed on many occasions, is direct sterilization, whether of the man or of the woman, whether permanent or temporary.[17]

Perhaps the opened windows of Vatican II set American Catholics up with unrealistic expectations. Accustomed to a steady diet of reform in the liturgy, in the clergy, and in parish structures, married Catholics looked forward to a hoped-for relaxation of the Church's traditional teaching against artificial birth control. Pope Paul VI himself had formed a commission to study the issue, and their leaked deliberations only added to an optimism that was fueled by the secular culture's loosened sexual morality. With *Humanae Vitae*, the pope rejected the work of his own commission.

Humanae Vitae was the beginning of spiritual dichotomy as Catholics compartmentalized their personal morality from their public loyalty to the Church. The encyclical was widely disregarded, with some confessors encouraging husbands and wives to "follow their conscience" rather than follow official Church teaching. Couples who practiced artificial birth control still went to Communion, still sent their children to parochial school, and continued to be publicly involved in the life of their parish. Some cite *Humanae Vitae* as the end of Catholic innocence and naiveté. For some, the teachings of the Church were no longer obeyed without question.

Many observers point to the 1968 encyclical as the turning point for clerical and religious obedience. Some priests and nuns who were already beginning to question their vows saw *Humanae Vitae* as the proverbial last straw.

Ray Repp took a leave of absence from his seminary studies that summer, but most of his fellow Folk Mass composers stuck it out, at least for a few more years. Interestingly, most, if not all, of the original class of ordained or professed Folk Mass composers eventually left the religious life with the notable exceptions of Father Clarence Rivers, Sister Miriam Therese Winter, and Sister Suzanne Toolan. Paul Quinlan soon left the Jesuits; the five Dameans, all ordained in the early 1970s, eventually left the priesthood and married, as did Fathers Peter Scholtes and Jack Miffleton. Father Carey Landry would marry his songwriting collaborator, Sister Carol Jean Kinghorn. Germaine Habjan famously refused to wear a nun's veil on *The Tonight Show with Johnny Carson* when she was scheduled to appear shortly after leaving her community. Why this mass defection among America's pioneer Folk Mass composers?

Repp talked about his disenchantment. "At that time, I was having a lot of doubts, disagreeing with the Church on almost every issue. I was working with young adults on a campus and everybody was feeling so hopeful — until *Humanae Vitae* came out. And I thought: Do I really want to be a part of this institution? It had nothing to do with lacking or losing faith. I just didn't want to perpetuate this institution."[18]

"There was more of an openness to think outside of the box and outside of the rules, or to do things that were creative and experimental," Buddy Ceasar remembers. "I think not only in terms of celibacy but also in terms of the limitations of the role of the priest, and some of the restrictions that were there that I felt uncomfortable with. And we were singing around the country and gaining a broader perspective."[19]

Carey Landry expressed it directly. "In my case, it was because of the love that developed between Carol Jean (Kinghorn) and me, and the closeness that our ministry together brought us. I experienced a freedom in (music) ministry that I wasn't experiencing in the confines of my diocese."[20]

Is it fair to place the blame on *Humanae Vitae* for the upheaval in the American Catholic Church? Probably not. But it was certainly a catalyst that many priests and religious point to as the beginning of their "thinking outside the box."

Meanwhile, the guitars kept on strumming. One wouldn't know that a crisis was eating away at the Church when so many of its parishes were singing "It's a Brand New Day." Hope-filled liturgical folk songs were enlivening the traditionally mournful funeral liturgy. Repp's "I Am the Resurrection" and "Peace, My Friends" became a soothing balm at the funerals of young soldiers killed in Vietnam.

1968 was an especially busy year for Carey Landry. He played guitar at the Folk Mass at The Catholic University in Washington, D.C., helped parishes in the area to start up their own folk liturgies through his workshops, and led the folk group on Sunday evenings at Saint Luke Parish in McLean, Virginia — all on top of an already-demanding course of seminary studies.

It was at Saint Luke that Landry befriended Ethel Kennedy, who approached the seminarian after Mass one Sunday evening to express her appreciation for the enthusiastic efforts of the young musicians. Landry was touched by Mrs. Kennedy's words of encouragement, shared so soon after the tragic death of her husband, Senator Robert Kennedy. He got to know the family very well, and was delighted when Mrs. Kennedy asked his group to sing at the baptism of Rory Elizabeth Katherine, who was born six months after her father's assassination. Carey composed a special song for the occasion, "Song of Baptism," which was eventually published in the very first *Hi, God* record and songbook.

Sunday after Sunday, from his choir's vantage point near the sanctuary, Landry could see the Kennedy family at prayer, and they sang along enthusiastically with his folk group. He marveled at the faith of this family who had sacrificed so much for their country. As the first-year anniversary of Senator Kennedy's death drew near, Mrs. Kennedy knew she could depend on Carey to provide music for the Memorial Mass at Arlington National Cemetery.

"She wanted a choir of young people to lead the music at that first anniversary Mass on June 6, 1969," Landry remembers. "There must have been five or six thousand people right on the hillside overlooking the gravesite near the Eternal Flame. We were there, a choir of about sixty young people with guitars and other contemporary instruments. Ethel and I had worked out the music for the liturgy. In fact, my song, 'What Would You Have Us Do,' where I quoted Senator Kennedy, was one of the songs at that Mass."[21]

For the final song of the liturgy, Mrs. Kennedy chose her husband's favorite sacred song, "Battle Hymn of the Republic," which had been sung so memorably at both the funeral and at the Democratic National Convention. In the warm June evening, as twilight turned to dusk, Landry and his friends launched into this truly original American folk hymn.

> In the beauty of the lilies Christ was born across the sea,
> With a glory in his bosom that transfigures you and me.
> As he died to make men holy, let us live to make men free.
> Our God is marching on....[22]

As the folk choir sang the iconic refrain, something magical happened. The hills at Arlington seemed to come alive with the spirit of Robert Kennedy. Joining the already large group at the memorial were hundreds more who processed to the gravesite in a touching display of solidarity and support for the family and for everything Bobby stood for.

From all directions they came, young and old, black and white, men and women of every race, creed, and economic status, each one carrying a lit candle and singing "Glory, glory, hallelujah" with Landry's choir. Tears streamed down their faces as they continued to sing the hymn for another half hour, the crowd growing into several thousand. Arlington Cemetery became awash in a soft radiance that recalled the inaugural address delivered so long ago by another fallen Kennedy brother.

> The torch has been passed to a new generation of Americans…and the glow from that fire can truly light the world….[23]

For one brief shining moment, the young Americans on that holy hill could forget the decade's turmoil as liturgy and idealism converged.

The fire of Camelot blazed once again.

---

1. Kurlansky, Mark, *1968: The Year That Rocked the World* (New York: Random House Trade Paperbacks, 2004) 380.
2. King, Dr. Martin Luther, Jr., "I Have a Dream" speech at the Lincoln Memorial, Washington, DC, August 28, 1963.
3. *Time* magazine Special, *1968: The Year That Changed the World*, 68.
4. Flannery, Austin, OP, editor, *Vatican Council II: The Conciliar and Post-Conciliar Documents,* "Gaudium et Spes #39" (Collegeville, MN: Liturgical Press, 1984) 938. Also cited in the Preface for the Solemnity of Christ the King.
5. FEL artist Father Ian Mitchell was Episcopalian.
6. Phone interview with the author, August 17, 2005, from Encino, California.
7. Powell, Mark Allan, *Encyclopedia of Contemporary Christian Music* (Peabody, MA: Hendrickson Publishers, Inc., 2002) 329.
8. All Landry quotes in this section from an interview with the author, November 15, 2004, by phone to Indianapolis, Indiana.
9. Interview with the author, February 10, 2007, Beaverton, Oregon.
10. All Miffleton quotes in this section from an interview with the author, March 8, 2007, Martinez, California.
11. Interview with the author, December 18, 2004.
12. Interview with the author, November 5, 2004.
13. Interview with the author, January 6, 2006, New Orleans, Louisiana.
14. In 1977, original member Dave Baker left the Dameans and was replaced by Gary Daigle.
15. Caspary, Anita M., *Witness to Integrity: The Crisis of the Immaculate Heart Community of California* (Collegeville, MN: Liturgical Press, 2003) 186 ff.
16. *Los Angeles Times*, "Father DuBay to Wed a Divorced Mother of 4," August 9, 1968.
17. Pope Paul VI, *Humanae Vitae*, 9, 14.
18. Interview with the author, October 1, 2004, Portland, Oregon, by phone to Ferrisburg, Vermont.
19. Interview with the author, January 6, 2006, New Orleans, Louisiana.
20. Interview with the author, November 15, 2004, by phone to Indianapolis, Indiana.
21. Ibid.
22. Text by Julia Ward Howe (1819–1910).
23. Inaugural Address of President John. F. Kennedy, January 20, 1961.

Chapter Eleven
"Sing, People of God, Sing"

> When I was a teenager, the church was a circus. Everyone sang Top 40 tunes at Mass. It didn't matter if they were related [to the liturgy]. I remember once on Ascension Thursday, the day Jesus ultimately transcends this world and, body and soul, enters heaven, the hip hymn committee sang "Leaving on a Jet Plane."[1]
>
> —Seminarian Mark Dolson, from Bill C. Davis' *Mass Appeal* (1981)

Where did the term "Folk Mass" come from? No one knows for sure. It has been used throughout this book as a convenient moniker for the innovative use of folk music in the Roman liturgy. For better or for worse, "Folk Mass" is an instantly recognizable designation, but it was never universally accepted.

Many of the pioneer composers, including Ray Repp, never liked the term, preferring "Guitar Mass" or "Folk Guitar Mass" or "liturgies with folk-style music." Much of the literature of the day put the word in quotes — "folk" Mass — which made for annoying reading since quotation marks imply something that may not actually be valid. Maybe that was the point.

As we have seen, the US Bishops got around the issue by not naming any style of music in the 1967 "Church Music" document that approved the liturgical use of "music that is meaningful to persons of this [high school or college] age group." But it was quite clear that the bishops were addressing the use of folk-style music for Mass.

Jack Miffleton observed: "The very term 'Folk Mass' — I'm not sure when that came in because we never looked at it initially as some kind of Folk Mass. I think somebody must have named it that along the way, to make a distinction between a 'regular' parish Mass and the time when the kids somewhere were going to have this Mass with guitars. There were pejorative things that came from that — 'Hootenanny Mass,' for example — by people who were extremely uncomfortable in that medium.

"Initially, some of the music was written because of the social justice things going on at the time, and it really wasn't intended for Mass as such. We had the whole rediscovery of the Bible in the Catholic Church that was taking place then, too. We had the biblical studies at Baltimore (Saint Mary's Seminary) when I was there, with Raymond Brown[2] (1928–1998) and other groundbreaking professors. It was very exciting. And we had a lot of services that were called Bible Vigils, where we would read Scripture and sing songs. We could sing secular songs, too."[3]

Miffleton's point is well taken. The use of folk music to express religious ideas was not exclusive to the liturgy. Many of these new songs were composed for public performance at coffeehouses, political rallies, concert halls, non-liturgical prayer services, or in a religious education classroom, but not necessarily at Mass.

For example, Ray Repp originally composed his bouncy "Here We Are" for the children in a religious education class that he was teaching as a seminarian.

> Most of us remember what it felt like as students to go to class unprepared. Sometimes even teachers have the same feeling. Back in 1964, part of my training as a seminarian studying theology was to teach CCD [Confraternity of Christian Doctrine].[4] One day, on my way to teach a fourth grade class, I found myself in that awkward position (no preparation). In the five-minute drive from the seminary to the school my mind worked quickly to come up with material to fill the fifty-minute class. The product of these five minutes of effort was a song ["Here We Are"], which the fourth graders seemed to enjoy. I still remember their faces and enthusiasm.[5]

The problem was that publishers released these non-liturgical songs in hymnals and liturgical songbooks, prompting parish musicians to sing them at Mass. The folk repertoire was thin, and musicians were eager to get their hands on anything available. After all, it was published! Surely, that meant it was suitable for liturgy.

Another problematic area was the lack of training or ministerial formation for the parish Folk Mass musicians who, unlike their pre-Vatican II predecessors, had no tradition to support their efforts. If you could play four chords on a guitar, you automatically qualified as a liturgical musician. Folk music's easy accessibility attracted volunteers in droves, youth in particular, and that generated some unique dynamics. Composer Tim Schoenbachler (b. 1952) observed:

> A [folk] group usually met once a week to rehearse. The choice of that week's musical line-up was planned at the rehearsal, usually with little thought, creativity, or coordination involved. Choosing music at rehearsals wasted valuable practice time. Musicians got itchy waiting to begin. After the music was selected the group spent perhaps two hours working on their performance. Since most of them had no musical training, there was little creativity in arranging a musical piece — everyone strummed alike and dynamics were minimal.

> When the folk group walked out into the sanctuary, they came loudly. Standing before the congregation was a group of young kids with little musical and liturgical education. They were there to lead adults in an adult worship experience.

> Often, the congregation enjoyed just listening to the music. Congregational singing, however, was weak. This was due in part to a lack of leadership by the folk group, which was often only capable of worrying about keeping itself together.[6]

It wasn't just the fact of guitars at liturgy that shocked many people; it was also the way those guitars were played. Even on the earliest Folk Mass records, producers took care to create a compelling sound that utilized the full versatility of the instrument: finger-picking, colorful lead lines, and a variety of different strums, emulating the folk music sound heard on secular records. Such subtly was lost on many parish guitarists, who enthusiastically played the same basic strum on every song:

Strum-de-dum-de-dum, strum-de-dum-de-dum, strum-de-dum-de-dum, strum-de-dum-de-dum…

"Shout from the Highest Mountain" started this way. So did "Take Our Bread," "Hear, O Lord," and "The Living God." It was the signature rhythm of almost every 4/4 song in the Folk Mass repertoire, strummed with uniform abandon by every guitarist in the folk choir. And it drove some people nuts.

Thus, the music of the Folk Mass became an easy target of derision by musicians and liturgists. In order to look at this music critically, one needs to ask two questions: "Was it folk music?" and "Was it liturgical?"

In a recent interview from *Call to Action News,* folksinger Paul Stookey (b. 1937) of Peter, Paul & Mary fame shared his ideas on a definition for folk music:

> Folk music has two aspects: participation, not just by the musicians but also by the audience; and advocacy — an articulation of concerns that transcend entertainment. A folk song typically has a lot of lyrics. Audiences have to be with it enough to digest an overload of information. The applause after a folksong isn't simply for the musicians. It says, 'We agree with what you just said.' Or, an uncomfortable silence or even occasional boos show the pain of our nation's unresolved problems that surface as a song is sung.[7]

Pete Seeger, American folk music's senior statesman, has shared his observations of the genre.

> I feel that the more young musicians strive to master the finest folk traditions of the past, the better music they will make in the future. It took thousands of years to develop these traditions; let us not lightly think that we can improve upon them without considerable artistry.[8]

> We, the people, suffer by not having the songs we need — songs which will echo in poetic form the thoughts and experiences we've had. We need thousands of new songs these days, to poke fun at some of the damn foolishness going on in the world; songs of love and faith in mankind and the future; songs to needle our consciences and stir our indignation and anger.[9]

Given its fluid versatility, a clear definition of folk music is probably unattainable,[10] but Stookey and Seeger point to some key elements. Folk music empowers an audience to join with the musicians in singing songs that speak powerfully on the issues of the day. While the style is steeped in a music tradition that goes back several generations, new folk singers must continue to emerge as the voice and conscience of their own generation.

On the surface, the Folk Mass music seems to reflect the outlook of the secular folk singers. Certainly, the sheer catchiness of the genre's early songs enabled American Catholics to finally embrace congregational singing, but this was dependent on the quality of musicianship and the spirit of the community. Although seminaries and college campuses typically had Folk Masses where the assembly singing raised the roof, most parishes were less than successful. It is important to remember that prior to the Council, Catholics did not have a tradition of congregational singing. Composer Bob Hurd (b. 1950) comments:

"The Folk Mass succeeded insofar as its whole purpose was to provide music that the assembly could sing. And it did that better than the traditional music at the time. Currently, the assembly will sing the traditional hymns, which might now be judged as better music. They will sing those hymns because the folk guitar Mass brought the song into their mouths. Whereas in the old days, the choir would do the singing and the people would just stand there. From the point of view of implementing the Council's desire for the people to sing, the Folk Mass was a really tremendous thing."[11]

Lyrically, the Folk Mass songs were a mixed bag. The songs composed to specifically serve one of the four liturgical processions seem naïve by today's standards: "Here We Are" for the entrance song; "All That I Am" for the offertory; "Sons of God" for Communion; "The Mass Is Ended" for the recessional.

As discussed in Chapter Five, the Folk Mass repertoire probably shined its brightest when it directly addressed the social justice issues of the 1960s, reflecting the progressive papal encyclicals of the decade[12] and Jesus' own Gospel teaching on the kingdom of God. Repp's "Till All My People Are One," Rivers' "God Is Love," and Scholtes' "They'll Know We Are Christians" are examples of songs in which the composers expressed the conscience of their generation.

Also, the best songs of the early repertoire found their inspiration in biblical sources, e.g., Quinlan's many psalm settings. Although the Second Vatican Council encouraged Catholics to study the Bible, overturning hundreds of years of the opposite teaching, Scripture-based songs would not become the norm until the St. Louis Jesuits were published in the 1970s. What did emerge in many of the early Folk Mass songs was an entirely new lyrical content that blurred Catholic spirituality with 1960s secular humanism. Writer Mark Oppenheimer (b. 1974) explained this phenomenon.

> The music they [Folk Mass composers] wrote could make the Mass exciting and strange. Instead of sitting, standing, and kneeling, the new music might encourage swaying in a circle. The music might, on occasion, be

accompanied by interpretive dancing or drumming. And, perhaps most powerfully, the music provided opportunities for women to lead the congregation. Folk music is gender-blind. Women could play guitar and lead songs, just as men could.

Catholic folk songs also emphasized the primacy of intimate relations over distant, obedient ones — symbolism analogous to choosing lay leadership over clerical diktats. In the lay spirit of Vatican II, the God of these songs is kinder and gentler, more of a benevolent father than a judgmental overlord. Joe Wise makes this point by treating man's and woman's relationship with God as a partnership: "Yours as we stand at the table you set," he sings in "Take Our Bread." "We are the sign of your life with us yet."

Finally, Catholic folk songs encourage, in addition to naturalism and familiarity, a non-creedal universalism. Their religion is not about doctrine or catechism but about the generalized spirit. Whereas traditional Catholic liturgical music reminds people of the complexity and fanciness of Catholic ritual, these folk songs could easily be sung in a Methodist, Lutheran, or Presbyterian Church.[13]

It came as no surprise that many Protestant denominations took an immediate liking to the songs of the Catholic Folk Mass and incorporated them into their own worship services. In this ecumenical and humanist sense, the songs of the Folk Mass truly became the people's music.

But was the music of the Folk Mass liturgical? Before rushing to judgment, one must keep in mind several important factors: a) Composers often wrote songs quickly to fill a given liturgical need because there was no library of suitable English-language hymns; b) to meet demand, publishers relaxed the standards that used to govern their publication choices; c) the informal nature of folk music lent itself well to creative innovation; and d) most liturgical music of the 1960s was, by and large, experimental, as was the English Mass itself, which did not become finalized until the promulgation of the *Missal of Pope Paul VI* in 1970.

Within this experimental framework, the Council did not offer many guidelines for the Folk Mass composers to rely on. Capuchin Father Edward Foley (b. 1948), noted liturgist, points out:

In 1963, the *Constitution on the Sacred Liturgy* [*Sacrosanctum Concilium*] asserted that music performs a particular ministerial function in worship and forms a necessary or integral part of the liturgy (*CSL* 112). This statement was the culmination of almost sixty years of evolution in official Church opinions on Church music stretching back to Pius X, who maintained that music was an integral part of the solemn liturgy. By incorporating this revolutionary perspective into a document calling for the renewal of the liturgy, the *CSL* did more than simply reassert an old claim. Rather, it signaled the transformation of the church's worship music. It is notable, however, that the *CSL* offered few other principles to guide the transformation process.[14]

The document "The Place of Music in Eucharistic Celebrations," issued in November 1967 by the Bishops' Committee on the Liturgy (BCL),[15] made a guidelines breakthrough by naming "three judgments" for good liturgical music.

> 1. *The musical judgment.* Is the music technically and aesthetically good? This question should be answered by competent musicians. This judgment is basic and primary. The musician has every right to insist that the music used be good music; but when this has been determined, there are still further judgments to be made.
>
> 2. *The liturgical judgment.* The nature of the liturgy itself will help to determine what kind of music is called for, what parts are to be preferred for singing, and who is to sing them.[16]
>
> 3. *The pastoral judgment.* The pastoral judgment must always be present. It is the judgment that must be made in this particular situation, in these concrete circumstances. Does music in the celebration enable those people to express their faith in this place, in this age, in this culture? … The signs of the celebration must be accepted and received as meaningful. They must, by reason of the materials used, open up to a genuinely human faith experience. This pastoral judgment can be aided by sociological studies of the people who make up the congregation, studies which determine differences in age, culture and education, as they influence the way in which the faith is meaningfully expressed.[17]

The three judgments were sound principles that would be further developed in the 1972 BCL document "Music in Catholic Worship," but in the 1960s these guidelines were generally unknown. Until the formation of such groups as the Federation of Diocesan Liturgical Commissions (FDLC) in 1968 and the National Association of Pastoral Musicians (NPM) in 1976, composers and parish musicians pretty much fended for themselves, perhaps taking to heart the cry of the Celebrant from Leonard Bernstein's musical theater piece, *Mass*: "Make it up as you go along, lauda, laude…."[18]

The music of the Folk Mass was a living example of the long-raging theological debate on the sacred and the secular as a central dichotomy for religion.[19] Of this tension, Spiritan Father Lucien Deiss (1921–2007), internationally acclaimed liturgical composer, commented:

> Up to now, liturgical music seldom left the church. When, in some instances, it did leave, it quickly scurried to the safety of a concert hall. Similarly, "pop" music never found its way into the church. In fact, a sort

of racial segregation existed in regard to the two kinds of music. Moreover, this apartheid was upheld by official documents and was quite easily accepted by a great majority of the faithful. The Church had its own music, just as it had its own language, architecture, ornaments, and way of life. To the faithful, only "church songs" were appropriate in church; other songs, in which they honestly and fully expressed themselves, were only appropriate outside of church. But today, since the *Pastoral Constitution on the Church in the Modern World*, the church no longer wishes to confront the world, but, rather, chooses to put herself *into the world of today* (ecclesia *in* mundo hujus temporis). The Constitution states:

> Let the Church also acknowledge new forms of art which are adapted to our age and are in keeping with the characteristics of various nations and regions. Adjusted in their mode of expression and conformed to liturgical requirements, they may be introduced into the sanctuary when they raise the mind to God. (*Gaudium et Spes* 62)

The encounter between the music of "today's world" and the music of tradition should result in a new creation. Neither of these two kinds of music will remain exactly the same as it was before, but will be enriched by the other.[20]

The answer to the question "Was the music of the Folk Mass liturgical?" can only be answered fairly within its immediate post-Conciliar context. This music served its time well, but faded as the experimentation of the 1960s gave way to more standardized liturgical forms. It is no accident that most of the music of the Folk Mass era is no longer sung today, except for a handful of songs.[21] Catholic songwriting would grow and mature as contemporary liturgical music became mainstream. But there was one more landmark event of the Folk Mass era that would have a lasting impact not only on Catholic worship but also on the music industry at large.

---

1   Davis, Bill C., *Mass Appeal* (New York: Dramatists Play Service, Inc., 1981, 1982, 2002) 19.
2   Sulpician Father Raymond Brown was a leading Catholic Scripture scholar who was a contributing editor of *The New Jerome Biblical Commentary*.
3   Interview with the author, March 8, 2007, Martinez, California.
4   Confraternity of the Christian Doctrine (CCD) was the official name of the parish program organized to teach religion to public school children.
5   Repp, Ray, "A Personal Odyssey and Observation," *Pastoral Music*, April-May 1984, 8:23–25.
6   Schoenbachler, Timothy, *Folk Music In Transition: The Pastoral Challenge* (Glendale, Phoenix, AZ: Pastoral Arts Associates of North America, 1979) 17–18.
7   Blumenkemper-Grindstaff, Laura, "What Do CTA and Peter, Paul and Mary Have In Common?" *Call to Action News*, Volume 26, Number 1, April 2004.
8   Seeger, Pete, *The Incompleat Folksinger* (New York: Simon and Schuster, 1972) 62–63.
9   Ibid., 157.

10 "At the other end is the definition of the late Big Bill Broozny, the blues singer. He was asked if a certain blues he sang was a folk song. 'It must be,' he replied. 'I never heard horses sing it.'" From Seeger, Pete, ibid, 62.
11 Interview with the author, July 21, 2005, San Jose, California.
12 Pope John XXIII wrote *Pacem in Terris* (Peace on Earth, 1963) and *Mater et Magistra* (Christianity and Social Progress, 1961); Pope Paul VI wrote *Populorum Progressio* (Progress of Peoples, 1967).
13 Oppenheimer, Mark, *Knocking On Heaven's Door: American Religion in the Age of Counterculture* (New Haven and London: Yale University Press, 2003) 78–80.
14 Foley, Edward, Cap., "Overview of Music in Catholic Worship and Liturgical Music Today," from *The Liturgy Documents: A Parish Resource, Volume 1* (Chicago: Liturgy Training Publications, 1991) 270.
15 "Bishops' Committee on the Liturgy" became the new name of the Commission of the Liturgical Apostolate on February 1967.
16 A discussion on liturgical text requirements follows, along with a list that prioritizes the various liturgical texts: a. Readings; b. Acclamations (Holy, Alleluia, Amen); c. Psalms and Hymns; d. Prayers.
17 McManus, Frederick R., editor, *Thirty Years of Liturgical Renewal: Statements of the Bishops' Committee on the Liturgy* (Washington, DC: United States Catholic Conference, Inc., 1987) 99–100.
18 "A Simple Song," ©1971 Leonard Bernstein and Stephen Schwartz.
19 The dichotomy was identified by French sociologist Emile Durkheim in his 1912 book, *The Elementary Forms of Religious Life*. "In Durkheim's theory, the sacred represented the interests of the group, especially unity, which were embodied in sacred group symbols and totems. The profane, on the other hand, involved mundane individual concerns." From Pals, Daniel, *Seven Theories of Religion* (New York: Oxford University Press, 1996) 99.
20 Deiss, CSSP, Lucien, *Spirit and Song of the New Liturgy* (Cincinnati, OH: World Library of Sacred Music, 1970) 237.
21 The short list of Folk Mass-era songs still in use today includes "Look Beyond" by the Dameans; "I Am the Bread of Life" by Mercy Sister Suzanne Toolan; "They'll Know We Are Christians" by Peter Scholtes; "Make Me a Channel of Your Peace" by Sebastian Temple; and "Into Your Hands" by Ray Repp (primarily not in English but in Spanish as "Entre Tus Manos").

Chapter Twelve
"Glory Land"

Tip the world over on its side and everything loose will land in Los Angeles....[1]

—Frank Lloyd Wright

Then it suddenly occurred to me that, in all the world, there neither was nor would ever be another place like this City of the Angels. Here the American people were erupting, like lava from a volcano; here, indeed, was the place for me — a ringside seat at the circus.[2]

—From *Southern California Country* by Carey McWilliams

FEL Publications had come a long way from its beginnings in Mary Sandifur's living room when a handful of friends frantically put together the 1963 mailing of the *Demonstration English Mass* record and missal. Dennis Fitzpatrick stayed true to his vision and brought about significant change in the liturgical life of the American Catholic Church. His musical talent, aggressive marketing, and sheer chutzpah helped make the vernacular liturgy a reality. His discovery and promotion of Ray Repp and other young composers brought a second revolution in the popularization of the Folk Mass. What would this forward-thinking publisher do next?

In January 1967, Fitzpatrick was invited by the Bishops' Commission on the Liturgical Apostolate to join its Music Advisory Board as a publisher representative. This great honor, which Fitzpatrick readily accepted, was not so much a concession to the burgeoning Folk Mass movement as it was an acknowledgment of his expertise and experience from the early days of liturgical reform.

The correspondence between Fitzpatrick, Father McManus, Archabbot Weakland (b. 1927), and other board members reveals much discussion on such issues as guidelines for diocesan music commissions, the ongoing translations of liturgical texts from the original Latin, musical settings of the Our Father, hymn substitution for the Propers of the Mass, the possibility of an official national hymnal and, as early as June 1967, the problem of copyright violation by the parishes. Fitzpatrick was involved in the discussions that led to the landmark US bishops document, "The Place of Music in Eucharistic Celebrations," with its groundbreaking "three judgments" for good liturgical music.[3] Although the Music Advisory Board did not spend too much time addressing the Folk Mass movement, Fitzpatrick's status as a member emboldened his progressive agenda.

∙■∙

FEL needed to expand, especially after the phenomenal success of *Hymnal for Young Christians*. Demand was increasing from around the country for appearances by their growing roster of composers and artists. There had never been a need to promote composers in the Latin Mass days, but now Catholic publishers assumed the trappings of the secular recording industry, including the public relations machinery. FEL's press releases were textbook examples of record industry copy, filled will hyperbole, colorful adjectives, and unabashed commercial promotion:

> For Immediate Release:
> MILWAUKEE TO "COME ALIVE" WITH RAY REPP
>
> Ray Repp <u>in person</u> at Liturgical Week!!
>
> This talented composer, whose music and voice make audiences come alive, will headline the exciting FEL Liturgical Week Concert, Wednesday, August 27, 10:15 PM, Sheraton-Schroeder Hotel, Milwaukee.
>
> ...Other concert headliners include: The Dameans, a quintet of "swinging seminarians" from New Orleans; Baptist Folksinger and Composer John Fischer; Fr. [Ian] Mitchell, the Episcopalian priest and his charming wife, Caroline; and the ghetto rock group from St. Brendan's Parish, Chicago, singing the popular hymn, "They'll Know We Are Christians."[4]

With so much success under his belt, Fitzpatrick felt the time was right for the company to move to Southern California. In 1967, FEL set up shop at 1543 West Olympic Boulevard, just a few blocks from the Chancery office of the Archdiocese of Los Angeles.

"The two most powerful [American] clerics were [Cardinals] Cody and McIntyre. And I thought I would take them both on," Fitzpatrick recalls. "That's why I went to Los Angeles. I thought the popularity of the Folk Mass music would spread, so I wanted to have the presence of two offices."[5]

Certainly, the conservative Archdiocese of Los Angeles was behind the Midwest in many respects, particularly in the liturgy. Roger Nachtwey recalled his utter amazement when, in 1968, he and Thomas Cook attended their first Sunday liturgy in Los Angeles at Immaculate Conception Church, adjacent to the Chancery office. They were shocked to find the priest was still celebrating Mass facing the wall! The folks at FEL had their work cut out for them.

"The archdiocese was so backwards they didn't even know who I was," Fitzpatrick remembers. "So they didn't really bother me much at all."[6] Folk Masses were not yet officially approved for the parishes, but many priests celebrated them at home liturgies and underground Masses. Characteristically, when the archdiocese banned the use of the liberal Dutch Catechism, Fitzpatrick made sure it was available for sale at FEL.

"We knew a number of priests from Los Angeles who had attended different events at Friendship House in Chicago when I was director of education there," said Cook. "They had come out to weekend programs with us where we used FEL music, so they were familiar with it. So we had some sense of a base to begin with. We figured the L.A. area was ripe for the folk music and it turned out to be true.

"We got to know many priests, especially those who were being called to the Chancery [for disciplinary reasons] by Cardinal McIntyre. They'd get bawled out by the cardinal, then came down the street to our office and tell us what had happened while they bought some music. As a matter of fact, I forget who it was, but some priest friend went to St. Basil's Church (where the cardinal resided), took McIntyre's nameplate from his confessional and attached it to my office door! That was the kind of rapport we had with the local clergy."[7]

Despite rumors to the contrary, the L.A. archdiocese never issued an outright ban of FEL's music or the use of folk music in the parishes. "People came to that conclusion but there wasn't any official policy on it," said Father Peter Nugent (b. 1936), former assistant director of the archdiocesan music commission. The guidelines issued on September 18, 1968, were accepted by Cardinal McIntyre and included a list of "approved" songs, including Jan Vermulst's "Guitar Mass" (World Library); Cyril Reilly's "Mass in Honor of St. Thomas More" (FEL); the music of Sister Suzanne Toolan (GIA), Father Lucien Deiss (World Library), and several other composers, plus the hymn "They'll Know We Are Christians."[8] Most glaring on the approved list was the absence of any work by Ray Repp.

In a statement to the *Los Angeles Times*, Fitzpatrick said the guidelines were "cautious first steps, but encouraging. Still, they ignored some major composers in the field who enjoy greatest popularity among young Catholics."[9] FEL promptly sent out a mailing that included a leaflet for Reilly's Mass setting, samplers of approved songs such as "They'll Know We Are Christians," and Robert Blue's arrangement of the traditional "Let Us Break Bread Together."

The new guidelines were hailed as a victory for FEL and lovers of the Folk Mass throughout Southern California despite the fact that some of the most nationally popular songs were not included. But the dam had opened a crack and no one could stop the torrent of fresh music that poured forth. The approved list was simply ignored as folk choirs sang whatever they wanted. At the archdiocese's Queen of Angels High School Seminary, seminarians were often taken to task whenever they sang a Ray Repp song at their class liturgies. Thus emerged the amusing spectacle of the innocent children's song "Here We Are" becoming a song of protest for teenagers defying a faculty member's suppression.

By 1968 FEL's staff had increased. Supporting Fitzpatrick were Jim Schaefer (director of publications), Fran Farber (agency division — workshops, composer appearances, public relations), Thomas Cook (administrative aide), and Roger Nachtwey (music editor). John Kellogg, Fitzpatrick's brother-in-law, remained involved as an advisor to the company. Fr. Richard Means of the Archdiocese of Chicago was brought on board as "religious advisor." The perception of FEL as a major music company was underlined by the hiring of Leroy G. Kanapaux as vice president of FEL/Flair Records. Previously with Herder and Herder, Inc., of New York, Kanapaux's FEL appointment was noted in the October 4, 1969 edition of *Billboard* magazine.

As popular as FEL and the Folk Mass had become,[10] a shared concern affected all Catholic music publishers: they were not earning their hoped-for profits. The cause was the widespread illegal copying and distribution of their lyrics and music.

"The problem was that I owed money," said Fitzpatrick. "I couldn't get out of [the business] even if I wanted to because I owed a lot of bills. And then I thought 'Why do I owe a lot of money? I should be making some money.' And that's when I discovered the illegal copying. I did some surveys and even I was blown away by the amount of illegal copying. I had no idea it was as high as it was. And I think the number was something like 78% of the copies being used was illegal."[11]

There are two factors to consider here. First, there is the very nature of folk music. Although the great songs of Pete Seeger, Woody Guthrie, and their cohorts were published and copyrighted, there was an almost an implicit approval of the music being copied and shared through the primitive technologies of the time: radio, tape recordings, and mimeograph, as well as the hearts and memories of the people who sang along. Folk music was the people's music — empowering, accessible, and free. Since the trendy soundtrack of the post-Conciliar Church was based on folk music, it was natural for this informal sharing to permeate the distribution of liturgical music.

This attitude leads to our second consideration, the suspension of moral obligation by parish leadership when it came to music. The Folk Mass took off like wildfire across America, fueled by inexpensive ditto and mimeograph printing. It was simply a matter of copying lyrics and chords, since the folk melodies were catchy enough to be learned at first hearing. Parish priests, nuns, school teachers, folk group leaders, and musicians had no compunctions about distributing homemade illegal copies of "Make Me a Channel," "Of My Hands," "Gonna Sing, My Lord," "They'll Know We Are Christians," or other Folk Mass favorites. After all, this music was for God! Anyone who challenged the legality of making copies for Mass was probably old-fashioned and needed to get with the program. Compounding this problem was the lack of experience at the parish level of paying to support the liturgy. Pastors, accustomed to a volunteer choir that sang at the parish High Mass, were reluctant to allocate any funds in support of these teenagers and their guitars.

The publishers tried to make it easy for parishes to use liturgical folk music by introducing the loose-leaf hymnal, which enabled churches to purchase only those songs that they wanted and insert them in their own custom-made binders. World Library's Dave Island (b. 1931), now with OCP, recalls, "It was a collaborative idea with Omer Westendorf, myself, and others. I think some other publishers had started something similar, but we really went to town with it." Thus, in 1968 their popular *People's Mass Book* was released in loose-leaf format in a green binder.[12]

It seemed like a good idea, generating unprecedented cooperation among the three major publishers,[13] who all agreed to print and cut their single song sheets in the same size: 5 inches by 7.5 inches, with a 12-hole square perforation. FEL called their version the *Custom Hymnal* and boldly proclaimed in a color brochure:

> BECOME YOUR OWN EDITOR! Now you can edit that perfect hymnal for a "truly pastoral celebration." No editor from any publishing house can choose hymns for your congregation as well as you can…. If you have ever copied an author's words or a composer's music, you have taken legitimate income from him, even if it was for a good cause…. Help us right this wrong by using the *Custom Hymnal* sheets….[14]

Customers were at first ecstatic. Finally, at only 3.5 cents per sheet, here was an affordable way for a parish to create the hymnal that they needed. With this loose-leaf format it was possible to have a worship resource that included the songs of almost any composer who was published by the "Big Three." In one liturgy, an eclectic parish could now lawfully sing Ray Repp's "Allelu" for the entrance song, Jan Vermulst's "Mass for Christian Unity" for the parts of the Mass, Joe Wise's "Take Our Bread" for the offertory, Joseph Gelineau's "My Shepherd Is the Lord" for Communion, and Martin Luther's "A Mighty Fortress Is Our God" for the recessional. Such variety! It was a liturgist's dream come true. Unfortunately, it became a publisher's nightmare.

"We had hundreds of cubbyholes, all with single pages in them," Dave Island recalls. "We got an order for X number of titles and had to go through by hand and get these all out. It was pretty labor-intensive, and the manual cost of putting all the selections together with each customized order was killing us. It was also an inventory nightmare, trying to guess what song would be the most popular. Pages would get torn out and people would re-order three of this, 25 of that, 16 of this. It just got impractical."[15] The loose-leaf hymnal died quietly after a few short years.

Seeking other ways to curb illegal copying, FEL had a brief flirtation with color printing. Without warning, *Hymnal for Young Christians* and other songbooks were printed with black or green ink on grey stock paper, or, most glaringly, red ink on goldenrod paper. This rainbow product was indeed hard to photocopy, but it was also hard to read, even under optimum lighting. Trying to read the music in darkened, poorly lit churches was next to impossible.

The general public was aghast at these changes and the company lost additional money as dissatisfied customers returned large orders. It also didn't help that photocopy technology was improving exponentially. No sooner had FEL published a work in green-on-gold paper then the Xerox Company released an advanced machine capable of making clear copies from color originals. The rainbow experiment was a failure.

In November 1972, FEL unleashed the most daring concept of all in its ongoing struggle with illegal copying: the "Annual Copy License," allowing unlimited usage of any or all of the company's 1,250 copyrights for an annual fee of $100.[16] This broke down to less than $2 per Sunday. Fitzpatrick explained the program in his letter to the customers that year:

> In worship, we all have discovered the impact of the Xerox machine and other forms of copying, along with the use of slides, transparencies, and overhead projectors.... It follows, then, that traditional publishing is superfluous, out-of-date, and far too restrictive. Rather, what is needed from a publisher is an enlightened and, indeed, an enthusiastic licensing policy that encourages a worship leader to take advantage of the timeliness and flexibility that copying devices offer, with as little bother as possible.[17]

Liturgical musician Maggie Hettinger, of the Archdiocese of Louisville, commented on parish reaction to FEL's innovative licensing policies in her 2000 essay on Ethics and Leadership:

> The Annual Copy License allowed parishes to make unlimited copies of the songs for a period of one year at a cost of $100, renewable at the end of the year for $100. FEL also offered Prior Copying Release that would excuse past copyright infringement for a single payment of $500. This is a familiar concept now, but needs to be put into historical perspective. At that time the entire hymnal sold for 39 cents. In churches that had never before provided worship aids for the assembly, neither having such a process nor even having dreamed of setting a budget for such things, to pay the princely sum of $600 for something they already had would have been incomprehensible.[18]

The Annual Copy License was an innovative effort on FEL's part, and many parishes and dioceses jumped on the licensing bandwagon enthusiastically. However, the hoped-for majority compliance was unrealized. The company needed a more radical strategy to meet its expenses and pay its composer royalties. As a cost-cutting measure, Fitzpatrick shuttered FEL's Midwest office in 1971. But FEL was not yet finished with the Archdiocese of Chicago.

· ■ ·

Gary Ault remembers *Walk to That Glory Land*, the Dameans' third collection of songs, as ill-fated from the start. Produced by Jim Schaefer, it was recorded in Los Angeles with the finest Hollywood talent, under the leadership of Ed Lojeski, a noted motion picture music arranger who recruited a veritable Who's Who of studio musicians, including Larry Knechtel, who was fresh off a Grammy win for his piano work on Simon and Garfunkel's "Bridge Over Troubled Water." By this time, the Dameans had become FEL's most popular artists, playing to standing-room-only crowds at catechetical conferences and parish concerts around the country. Their much-anticipated 1971 release, a showcase for the group's maturity as composers, surely deserved red-carpet treatment.

However well intentioned, this professional production strategy was flawed in two important aspects. First, the Dameans had no say in how their well-crafted songs would sound on their own record, bucking the then-current trend in the secular music industry of allowing singer-songwriters and rock groups to arrange and produce their own albums. Secondly, the extravagant expense of *Glory Land's* production would be deducted from the Dameans' royalties, meaning that the artists wouldn't see a single penny from the sales of their new record until well into their dotage.

The deduction of recording and distribution costs from artist royalties was a standard clause in the secular recording artist contracts utilized by FEL. The problem, however, was the differential in scale between the two music worlds. The recording costs of secular artists, although the same as for liturgical artists, could be spread over the sales of hundreds of thousands of units. Liturgical artists, at best, sold only several thousand records. This was not a problem for the simple recording techniques used for Ray Repp's seminal *Mass for Young Americans*, but cost recovery became an impossible hurdle for the Dameans' lavish production.

Ault and his fellow Dameans couldn't believe their ears when they heard what Ed Lojeski had done to their songs. The title track was originally written with a gospel feel, but the Hollywood arranger made it sound like a television theme song. Dave Baker's "Love Is Patient" was given the "Nashville Sound" treatment, complete with pedal steel guitar. The tempo of many songs was quickened and "enhanced" using the over-busy electric bass style popular in the early '70s. "In My Name," Darryl Ducote's moving ordination ballad, was scored with a treacly string ensemble reminiscent of the theme song from a gothic movie. The overlooked point in this production was that, unlike their previous albums, the arrangements of *Walk to That Glory Land* were not liturgical and could not be duplicated by the Dameans in concert.

"We fought Ed on almost every track," recalls Ault. "We did manage to tone down the arrangements on a few songs, but for the most part the slick Hollywood production values prevailed. This was not the Dameans sound. We threw our hands up and walked away from the studio in frustration. I know I didn't want to have anything to do with this album again."[19]

The album cover added insult to injury. A cartoonist had been commissioned to design the graphics, and the purple-on-white rendering of the kingdom of heaven was considered odd, even in the context of late-1960s psychedelia. The words of the title were inverted, to be read from the bottom up as one symbolically took the walk suggested by Ault's imagery. Unfortunately, most people automatically read the words from the top down, rendering the album's title as *Land Glory That to Walk*.

Glory Land did receive some positive reviews. Henry Roth, music critic for *The Tidings* newspaper of the Archdiocese of Los Angeles, hailed it as "an extraordinary disc in the religious rock field."

> Their 10-tuner has unusual scope and variety. Support from a group of top Hollywood recording musicians lends a professional aura that is not always present in such enterprises.… Should attract wide interest among religious-oriented youth who cotton to the 'mod' sound.[20]

Glowing reviews aside, the seeds of discontent had been sown among the five Dameans. They would never again record for FEL Publications. Indeed, the whole *Glory Land* project opened their eyes to perceived inconsistencies that would come back to haunt their publisher eight years later in a Baton Rouge, Louisiana, courtroom.

---

1 Quoted in Wright's obituary, April 9, 1959.
2 McWilliams, Carey, *Southern California Country*, (New York: Duell, Sloan & Pearce, 1946) 376.
3 Cf., chapter 11's discussion on this document.
4 FEL press release, August 1969.
5 Interview with the author, May 15, 2004, Las Vegas, Nevada.
6 Interview with the author, May 15, 2004, Las Vegas, Nevada.
7 Interview with the author, December 28, 2003, Los Angeles, California.
8 "LA Archdiocese Authorizes Guitar and Folk Music Masses," *Los Angeles Times,* September 19, 1968.
9 Ibid.
10 According to Fitzpatrick, the company's attorneys estimated that 71% of the Catholic liturgical market was using the FEL's music in the early 1970s.
11 Interview with the author, May 15, 2004, Las Vegas, Nevada.
12 Interview with the author, May 26, 2004, Portland, Oregon.
13 FEL, World Library of Sacred Music, and GIA were the major Catholic music publishers of the late 1960s.
14 FEL marketing brochure, 1968
15 Interview with the author, May 26, 2004, Portland, Oregon.
16 Approximately $500 in 2008 dollars.
17 FEL brochure, 1972.
18 Hettinger, M., An Ethical Spotlight on Unauthorized Copying of Liturgical Music with the Catholic Church, dissertation, December 21, 2000.
19 Interview with the author, January 6, 2006, New Orleans, Louisiana.
20 Roth, Henry, *The Los Angeles Tidings,* October 15, 1971.

Chapter Thirteen
The Time Has Not Come True

When asleep, we dream a lot
about the things we haven't got when morning comes.
Morning goes and afternoon,
and all the light is gone so soon, and nothing's done.
There are things we want to do,
but then we fall asleep to dream again.
And the days are growin' shorter for us.
Still we all can hope it's not too late.[1]

—Ray Repp

Before 1964, Catholic publishing served niche needs: personal missals, devotional booklets, catechisms, and spiritual reading. The *St. Gregory Hymnal* and the *St. Basil Hymnal* provided enough repertoire for parish choirs and organists whose performance opportunities were generally limited to Sunday High Mass, Wednesday Marian devotions, and Lenten Stations of the Cross. Congregational participation was not the norm, although Catholics of a certain generation have fond memories of singing "Hail, Holy Queen Enthroned Above" and the three Benediction hymns: "O Salutaris Hostia," "Tantum Ergo Sacramentum," and "Holy God, We Praise Thy Name."

All of that changed with the promulgation of the vernacular liturgy, and many publishers were caught by surprise. With music encouraged at every liturgy, not just at the High Mass, new repertoire was needed almost immediately. Those companies who did not move with the times were left behind in the dust. The forward-thinking Omer Westendorf was ready with his *People's Mass Book*, a financial boon for World Library of Sacred Music. Dennis Fitzpatrick took a great risk with the unproven music of Ray Repp, and FEL Publications became the trend-setting leader of the exploding Folk Mass movement.

New hymns, new composers, new music styles, new media, new publishing formats — everything was new as the old business models were tossed aside like last Friday's fish sticks. Catholic publishers were now dealing with recording studios, record pressing, artist contracts, royalty computation, concert promotion, and other details undreamed of in the pre-Vatican II days. The Folk Mass era was an exciting and colorful time of seemingly endless possibilities, reflecting well the changing Catholic Church. But near the decade's end, Church leadership began to pull on the reigns, and Catholic publishers would soon face an implosion.

The beginning of the industry's downturn may have been the suppression of the national Liturgical Week. Sponsored by the Liturgical Conference, this annual gathering began in 1940 under the guidance of such pioneers as Msgr. Reynold Hillenbrand. Reaching its apex with the 1964 gathering in St. Louis that featured the first official English Mass, the Liturgical Weeks became the most prominent concert venue for the new Folk Mass composers. Ray Repp, Clarence Rivers, Sister Germaine, Joe Wise, Paul Quinlan, the Dameans, and all their peers received valuable national exposure at this annual conference, and eager participants couldn't wait to get home and introduce the exciting new music to their parishes and campuses. But the Liturgical Week's liberal agenda was being viewed with increasing suspicion by certain influential bishops.

> Civil rights was the theme of the 1968 Liturgical week…and the theme was announced by the glitzy title: "Damn everything but the circus." The art of Corita Kent (1918–1986) was prominent in Washington's Shoreham Hotel where the meeting was held. Coretta Scott King (1927–2006) spoke in place of her slain husband amidst a carnival-like atmosphere that may have expressed more show than substance.
>
> The 1968 meeting was a success in many respects, but when Archbishop O'Boyle (1896–1987) of Washington found out that the Marxist historian Herbert Apthecker (1915–2003) was one of the speakers, he refused to come. Moreover, it was reported that priests at the Conference were changing some of the important wording of the Mass. At O'Boyle's request, the American bishops withdrew their Episcopal moderator from the Liturgical Conference in the fall of 1968.
>
> In the summer of 1969, the Liturgical Week was scheduled for Madison, Wisconsin. A month before the meeting, the priests of the Madison diocese were informed by their bishop that they were forbidden to participate because the Conference had no Episcopal status.[2]

With the marginalization of the Liturgical Conference, the Folk Mass composers and publishers lost an important forum. Since there was no formal Catholic radio network, contemporary Catholic artists relied, and still rely, on conferences like these to get new music into the hands of their target audience. Regional conferences, like the Los Angeles Archdiocese's Religious Education Congress in Anaheim, California, suddenly became hot concert venues. In 1976, the National Association of Pastoral Musicians (NPM), led by Father Virgil Funk (b. 1937), stepped in to fill the void left by the demise of the Liturgical Conference.

The downturn continued. In 1971, Omer Westendorf found himself on the wrong end of a large production bill, with no assets to cover it. After seeking the protection of Chapter 11 bankruptcy, World Library of Sacred Music was acquired by J.S. Paluch, an emerging missalette[3] publisher from Chicago. Although Westendorf's repertoire certainly raised the music selection in Paluch's *Monthly Missalette* by several notches, it would be years before World Library, now "a division of J.S. Paluch Company, Inc.," recaptured its innovative publishing spirit.

On the West Coast, FEL was forced to move out of its pleasant and strategically located office near the headquarters of the Archdiocese of Los Angeles because of a competing tenant who wanted their space. FEL's new location was at an industrial park in West Los Angeles, in a long one-room warehouse where seven staff members crowded into a small workspace in the midst of the inventory shelves. To his credit, Fitzpatrick did not seem to mind working in this cramped space with his staffers.

Other publishers entered the picture. North American Liturgy Resources (NALR), founded by Ray Bruno (formerly of World Library of Sacred Music), moved from Cincinnati to Phoenix and was trying to find its footing by publishing new, untried artists. Bruno's company and his family struggled financially for a few years. GIA Publications, an old-line Catholic publisher that hadn't fully embraced the Folk Mass trend, seemed to score a coup by releasing Sebastian Temple's *The Universe Is Singing*, a collection of the composer's reflections on the heady theological themes of Jesuit Father Teilhard de Chardin (1881–1955). Although intellectually provocative, none of this new music was suitable for liturgy and the album was not a big seller. Temple dropped out of the scene shortly thereafter.

Longtime observers of FEL couldn't help but notice that the company seemed to have lost its early momentum. Sister Germaine, Robert Blue, and John Fischer had gone on to other things and were no longer writing liturgical music. Ray Repp released his final FEL album in 1969, *The Time Has Not Come True*. The songs on this collection were not liturgical and not for group singing, but were of a much more personal nature, protesting what Repp saw as the flaws in modern society. Frustrated about several issues with the Church, Repp left the seminary and moved to Europe for three years, where he taught in an American school in Vienna and got involved in student anti-war protests.

Meanwhile, parishes continued to celebrate their Folk Masses, but the music selection was getting a little worn. The songs of Ray Repp, so vital and fresh in 1966, were considered old hat in 1972. Folk groups still enjoyed the Dameans, but their congregations wanted something new.

This was the time of the popular pseudo-religious musicals *Jesus Christ Superstar* and *Godspell*, and "Day by Day," the main production number from the latter, became a huge liturgical favorite. The Jesus People movement was in full swing, and their music found a home and focus at Calvary Chapel in Costa Mesa, California, leading to the founding of Maranatha! Publishing. This is often cited as a central catalyst for the Protestant Contemporary Christian Music industry, and some of these songs found their way into Catholic liturgy through the Charismatic Renewal, which had its beginnings at this time.[4]

As the decade progressed, NALR in Phoenix began to supply this need for new material with music by Paul Quinlan, who had moved on to NALR as a staff member;

Carey Landry; and a fresh group of young seminarians who were simply known as the St. Louis Jesuits.

Faced with these competitive threats, Jim Schaefer, director of publications, tried to lead FEL back to the forefront. He discovered the Roamin' Brothers, a group of American seminarians studying in Rome for the Oblates of Mary Immaculate. Schaefer and Roger Nachtwey went to Italy to record the group. The resulting album, *Listen to the Silence*, ended up being an expensive project that never yielded a much-needed new hit song or significant sales. A short while later, FEL released *Jesus Will Come Thru* by the duo Tom and Dan, who also failed to make an impression on Catholic liturgical music.

During this time, FEL continued its long-running songbook series, *Hymnal for Young Christians*. The third volume, compiled by Roger Nachtwey, was published in 1973. The inclusion of the popular songs from the recent Fischer and Dameans albums helped make *HYC III* desirable, but the table of contents revealed the names of mostly new composers who did not have a lasting impact on the liturgical market. The sole exception to this was Bob Hurd (b. 1950).

Hurd was a seminarian from St. John's College in Camarillo, California. Together with the theologate school, St. John's Seminary, this dual campus was the hub of priestly formation for the Archdiocese of Los Angeles. In 1971, Hurd was charged with coordinating the college folk liturgies, bringing to the position a passion for good music. He did not find much in the 1960's folk repertoire that his discerning community would want to sing, so Bob began composing original songs that reflected his considerable folk-rock musicianship and his generation's search for spiritual fulfillment.

Hurd's liturgical music rocked and became very popular with the seminarians. Their Sunday morning liturgy was open to the public and people in the surrounding Ventura County area would come from miles around to participate. Word got out that St. John's was the hot spot for outstanding contemporary worship, and the college chapel was filled every weekend with a standing-room-only congregation that sang with unabashed enthusiasm. Dennis Fitzpatrick visited St. John's one Sunday to see what all the fuss was about. Clearly impressed, he offered Hurd an exclusive contract to publish and record his songs. This resulted in two LP albums: *O Let Him In* and *Bless the Lord*.

Unfortunately, the Hurd albums were recorded on low budgets and rush-released, without much attention given to professional sound quality or comprehensive marketing. Although Hurd's music made a splash in Southern California, the suppression of the Liturgical Week conference resulted in the lack of a national forum to showcase FEL's new talent. Discouraged, Hurd briefly gave up composing. He left St. John's and went to De Paul University in Chicago to focus on his doctorate in philosophy. But his 1979 comeback album with Franciscan Communications, *Roll Down the Ages*, garnered national attention with its compelling mix of social justice themes and brilliant choral folk-rock sound. The composer found even greater success in the 1980s with Oregon Catholic Press. Today, Bob Hurd is a recognized leader in contemporary liturgical music.

・■・

There was irony in the fact that the early-1970s fallow period of Folk Mass publishing was in the wake of the new *Missal of Pope Paul VI*, promulgated on April 3, 1969, and implemented in the United States the following year. The period of liturgical experimentation was over, and the Mass was now entirely in the vernacular. The new missal introduced several innovations, including an expanded Lectionary with a three-year cycle of readings; three new eucharistic prayers and a simplified Roman Canon; four memorial acclamations to follow the institution narrative of the eucharistic prayer; and the dismantling of the old "High Mass" and "Low Mass" designations, with the encouragement to sing the ordinary Mass responses and acclamations at every liturgy.

The new Roman Missal opened up exciting possibilities for ritual music. The old four-hymn model was effectively retired, and new music was needed for the revised penitential rite; the responsorial psalm and alleluia; the memorial acclamations; and the new translations of the Glory to God, the Creed, the Holy, and the Lamb of God.

Unfortunately, some publishers didn't seem to understand this new music mandate and continued in the old model of just publishing stand-alone hymns. FEL, in the name of appealing to a more ecumenical audience, decided to stop publishing Mass settings and changed the meaning of its initials to "Faith, Evangelism, and Liturgy." World Library's parent company, J.S. Paluch, provided some new Mass settings in its popular *Monthly Missalette,* but musical monotony prevailed. The Mass propers, responsorial psalm and alleluia were all scored to be sung with Gregorian Psalm Tone VIII, and the innocuous "Danish Amen" was adapted as the featured melody for the remaining parts of the Mass. After several weeks of hearing endless variations on the same theme, even some conservative Catholics were longing for the strum-de-dum-de-dum rhythm of the early Folk Mass days.

This is the industry context in which FEL decided to pursue a strategy of ecclesial litigation.

As discussed earlier, the culture of copying was endemic in the secular folk music industry and this problem carried over into the liturgical world. Attempts to enforce parish copyright compliance — including FEL's innovative Annual Copy License — met with a tepid response. Fitzpatrick felt he had no choice except to threaten lawsuit to demonstrate the seriousness of the issue. He began gathering evidence of copyright infringement by conducting parish "surveys" in the archdioceses of Los Angeles and Chicago, and seventeen other dioceses.

In the summer of 1973, Fitzpatrick enlisted eight seminarians from St. John's Seminary College to visit the folk liturgies of numerous Los Angeles area churches and obtain any homemade hymnal used in the pews. The seminarians were paid a $5.00[5] bounty for each "pirated" hymnal they confiscated, and the "violations" piling up in the FEL office represented almost eighty churches. Most of these parish hymnals contained illegally reproduced lyrics of FEL's popular Folk Mass songs, with improper or no acknowledgment of composer credits or copyright dates.

Fitzpatrick followed up by sending a certified letter to the pastor of each Los Angeles parish allegedly infringing FEL copyrights, reiterating the $100-a-year Annual Copy License and demanding that the parish pay $100 for each previous year of violation. A letter was also sent to Timothy Cardinal Manning (1909–1989) explaining the problem and requesting a meeting to discuss possible settlement. The archdiocese initially offered a $16,000 settlement, far below the $30,000-plus that would be paid if the violating parishes complied with FEL's demands. Fitzpatrick declined the offer.

After additional negotiation, the matter settled when Cardinal Manning returned the problem back to the parishes by issuing a strongly worded letter from Msgr. Benjamin Hawkes (1919–1985), vicar general for the archdiocese.[6] Most parishes complied, some begrudgingly, and a few parishes opted to stop using FEL music altogether.

Father Donald Ruddy (d. 2000), pastor of St. Gregory the Great in Whittier, California, didn't mince words about the situation. "A group of teenagers put together a book of music they were performing at our 10:45 Mass. They weren't aware of the copyright laws and we used the book until Fitzpatrick got a hold of a copy and threatened to sue. Then I pulled it out. If I had my choice, I'd never use the stuff."[7] But FEL's action did bring significant copyright compliance throughout Southern California.

Impressed with the sheer number of violations and the initial success of the Los Angeles survey, Fitzpatrick conducted a similar operation in the Archdiocese of Chicago, enlisting his stepfather, his mother, and several of their friends to visit the folk liturgies of the local churches. Of the 182 parishes monitored in May 1976, 103 were found using FEL compositions without the appropriate permission.

The company strategy was more pointed in Chicago when Fitzpatrick was rebuffed in his attempts to effect a settlement similar to the one reached in Los Angeles. On September 20, 1976, FEL Publications filed suit against the Archdiocese of Chicago, charging John Cardinal Cody (1907–1982) and five Chicago-area churches (including Holy Name Cathedral) with 28 counts of copyright infringement.

> In the suit, Fitzpatrick estimated that his company has lost $29 million to alleged pirating nationwide over the past 10 years and that his 65 composers have been deprived of more than $500,000 in royalties in the last year alone. He estimated FEL's Chicago-area losses at more than $300,000 for the period.[8]

The Archdiocese of Chicago was taken by complete surprise, despite FEL hinting at possible lawsuits in its regular direct-to-parish mailings.[9] The attorneys for the archdiocese devised a legal defense that included a countersuit against FEL for "predatory acts and coercive tactics" and violation of various antitrust laws.

On the day of the filing, Fitzpatrick held a press conference in Chicago to introduce himself and present his case to the public. Msgr. Francis A. Brackin (d. 1987), the vicar general, issued a preliminary statement that seemed conciliatory: "If there is any infringement on his copyrights, we'll do whatever is necessary to correct it."[10] But Brackin soon employed a scorched-earth policy, sending a letter to every parish and ordering all FEL material, no matter how obtained, be removed from the churches, effectively banning the use of FEL music at all liturgies within the archdiocese. Over 300,000 parish hymnals were collected in plain cardboard boxes and stored in a warehouse for FEL to reclaim.

FEL retaliated by charging the archdiocese with harassment, since almost two-thirds of the collected material was properly licensed and the ban on performing FEL music constituted improper restraint of trade. US District Court Judge Alfred Kirkland agreed and ordered the archdiocese to return the confiscated hymnals to the parishes. Fitzpatrick claimed an early victory and, for a time, public opinion leaned to his side. Indeed, many Chicago parishes, angered by their archdiocese's strong-arm tactics, vowed to continue singing FEL's songs with the appropriate permission. The *National Catholic Reporter* championed FEL's cause, and Chicago Father Andrew Greeley (b. 1928) wrote passionately in FEL's defense in his nationally syndicated column.

> The suit filed by a major liturgical publishing company against the Archdiocese of Chicago (as a corporation sole) and a number of the more affluent parishes in the archdiocese for violation of the copyright laws is one of the major scandals of our day. It exposes a hypocrisy and an insensitivity to human rights which is shocking and disgraceful. One gets used to phoniness from ecclesiastics but the copyright case recalls Jesus' condemnation of the scribes and Pharisees....
>
> Let's be clear about it: This is robbery, indeed larceny on a grand and monumental scale. The clergy and religious who have violated the copyright laws have an obligation in strict justice not only to stop what they're doing but to restore in full what they have stolen.
>
> Don't hold your breath till that happens....[11]

Fitzpatrick was not willing to hold his breath. Realizing that FEL's case against the Archdiocese of Chicago might take years before final resolution (the final appeal decision was handed down on October 25, 1990), and buoyed by the early success, Fitzpatrick expanded his litigation strategy. On November 21, 1977, FEL filed a second suit charging the National Conference of Catholic Bishops (NCCB) and the U.S. Catholic Conference, Inc. (USCC)[12] with eighteen counts of copyright infringement and with unfair competition. Fifteen Catholic archdioceses and dioceses[13] were named in the complaint that sought damages of $8.6 million. The action against the NCCB was seen as a way to file suit against all Catholic dioceses in the United States.

In retrospect, any goodwill FEL gained in its early victory against the Archdiocese of Chicago dissolved with this second round of litigation. Many Catholics were upset with the idea of their bishops being sued on such a large scale. On May 18, 1978, attorneys for the NCCB were granted a motion to dismiss the FEL suit on the grounds that the NCCB/USCC enjoyed only "extremely limited" powers, restricted to the approval of acceptable vernacular texts for liturgical use, and that abuses in an individual diocese were the responsibility of the local bishop.

In the midst of this ongoing litigation, Fitzpatrick found time for his own creative musical outlet when he formed the English Chant Schola, a group of professional Los Angeles singers specializing in Gregorian chant performed in English. Starting with a modest Saturday evening Mass at Saint Sebastian Parish in West Los Angeles, the Schola grew in popularity when it moved to the UCLA Newman Center, where two local classical radio stations broadcast the group's weekly liturgies.

"These were actual Masses, but they broadcast it because of the quality of the music I was conducting," Fitzpatrick recalled. "I would compose some Ordinaries, and then I'd do some Byzantine Ordinaries, and then I would do Ralph Vaughan Williams' *Mass in G Minor*. It was magnificent work, in English. I did everything in English.

"I began to do the most complex of all the Gregorian chants: a different Gradual and different alleluia verse each time — the most virtuosic vocal music. And it was just magnificent. I have recordings of those. And people told me it was the highest art they had ever heard in the Catholic Church."[14]

Word of the English Chant Schola spread and soon Timothy Cardinal Manning requested the opportunity to preside at a radio liturgy with the Schola. Fitzpatrick had come full circle with the music that he loved. The English Chant Schola thrived for five fulfilling years.

Although the litigation continued, the publicity generated by FEL's lawsuits became a milestone for copyright compliance throughout the Church. Applications for the Annual Copy License grew tremendously, and bishops sent letters to their priests mandating that local parishes obtain permission before reprinting copyrighted music. Many sacred music publishers applauded Fitzpatrick's steadfast policies.

> "We knew there was a piracy problem before the FEL suit," said Frank Seigfried, president of Vanguard Music Corp., New York, "but it wasn't until after that we realized the extent. From the volume of mail we're now getting from Catholic churches requesting permission to use our music, I'd have to say it was sizable."
>
> Siegfried said he supports FEL's stand and thinks Fitzpatrick's $100 licensing plan is "an honest approach and an equitable offer."
>
> George Shorney, president of Hope Publishing Co., Chicago, said he believes the publicity surrounding the FEL suit "will benefit all of us in the sacred music industry." Shorney said his company sells primarily to a Protestant market and doesn't have an infringement problem of the same supposed magnitude as Catholic-oriented publishers.[15]

Predictably, no Catholic publisher would go on record in support of FEL's lawsuits of churches, although many did express anonymous gratitude for Fitzpatrick's temerity.

To all appearances, FEL was turning the corner and regaining its dominance in the industry, but its world was shattered in February 1979 when the Dameans filed suit against their publisher in the US District Court in Baton Rouge, Louisiana. Their central complaint was FEL's alleged non-payment of royalties from sales of the Dameans' records and printed music. *National Catholic Reporter* had a field day with the suit, making it a banner headline story for their newsweekly.

> That the accused is FEL has created a delicious irony in the minds of executives and observers of the religious music industry, an industry which may gross as much as $9 million annually.
>
> The observers remember the public stance taken by FEL president and founder Dennis Fitzpatrick when he filed suit [against the Archdiocese of Chicago] for alleged copyright violations: a mixture of piety and concern expressed mainly for his composers, rather than for his company.
>
> Now it is Fitzpatrick's FEL that is defendant in a suit regarding royalties — a suit whose attendant publicity clearly troubles him. He told *NCR* that people tend to believe "accusations made in print." He added, "I may have trouble signing people after this."[16]

According to the court record, the Dameans had three main allegations in their complaint: 1) FEL did not pay royalties to the group from at least $150,000 in sales of records and printed music; 2) FEL's contracts were one-sided and the company took advantage of young naïve artists; and 3) FEL failed to provide timely sales reports and to stock the stores with the Dameans' products.

In their complaint, the Dameans requested that the court return to them the ownership of their FEL copyrights; possession of the master tapes of their three FEL albums, *Tell the World, Songs of the New Creation,* and *Walk to That Glory Land*; and a payment of $75,000 as FEL's profit from their works.[17]

If the Dameans could prove their claims of FEL's tardiness in accounting reports and royalty payments it would constitute a breech of contract, but the complaint also painted a picture of contracts that were "one-sided to the point that (FEL) received virtually everything…and (the Dameans) received virtually nothing."

As seen in the previous chapter, the Dameans had their eyes opened with the *Walk to That Glory Land* recording sessions, in which the studio musicians were paid handsomely out of the artists' future royalties, which they would never see. The group was determined that this would never happen to them again.

FEL countered that the Dameans' "efforts to portray the contracts as one-sided in FEL's favor…absurd on their face." Not only did the group show the contracts to a lawyer before signing, FEL said, but also the group's members "were sufficiently satisfied with the contracts to enter into 15 of them over a three-year period." The tardy sales accounting was due to computer problems and the allegation of failure to supply stores adequately was based "only on the records of one bookstore in Baton Rouge."

At the August 1979 trial in Baton Rouge, the Dameans assembled an all-star group of witnesses: former FEL composers Robert Blue, (Sister) Germaine Kramlinger, Paul Quinlan, and Ray Repp. The composers were more than happy to testify on the Dameans' behalf. They also recruited the testimony of Jim Schaefer, the former director of publications for FEL who signed the Dameans to their contract in 1968.

As the trial began it became clear to FEL's attorneys that the company would not win this case. With resources already stretched thin because of the ongoing litigation in Chicago, FEL agreed to settle with the Dameans, granting them, among other things, ownership of their copyrights and master tapes. The Dameans went on to create new music for NALR and GIA Publications, re-releasing their three FEL albums with the latter. Eventually, the group re-recorded their FEL tracks, removing the overproduction that they felt was not reflective of their true group sound.

The importance of *Ault vs. FEL Publications* for the Catholic liturgical industry cannot be overstated. Catholic publishers learned from the FEL experience and the old system of expense deduction from royalties was eventually suppressed. Today's liturgical composers can thank the Dameans for the current contracts that allow for equitable royalty compensation within the unique contours of the Catholic market.

Dennis Fitzpatrick admits today: "I made a number of mistakes [with the shaping of artist contracts] that I would re-do if I had the opportunity to do it again. We just used the same contracts that RCA and the secular companies used. And maybe they were unfair but at the time I thought it was the industry standard, where you deduct the cost of recording before you pay royalties." When informed that today's Catholic publishers now pay for all artist recording and marketing expenses, Fitzptratick commented: "Good. The publishers are smart. It's a better way to do it."[18]

FEL Publications never recovered from its loss of the Dameans and the bad publicity of the trial. A few years later, Ray Repp took FEL to court and successfully won back his copyrights and master tapes. During the litigation years, FEL tried to maintain its mission as a vital liturgical music publisher by releasing the works of such new artists as Ron Griffen, Jim Shaw, Robert Rousseau, and a young seminarian named Ken Canedo (b. 1953). They also published a new folk hymnal called *SOAR (Sing Out, Arise and Rejoice)*. But the Dameans lawsuit was really FEL's death knell as a viable publisher. No new artist would want to sign up with "the litigation company."

On a brighter note, FEL expanded on its Annual Copy License with the creation of the Copyright Sharing Corporation. Conceived in 1977 by Dennis Fitzpatrick, CSC initially licensed over 2,000 copyrights from more than 144 authors and composers. The 11 participating publishers included American Catholic Press; Fred Bock Music Co.; FEL; In Sync, Inc.; Joral Records; Servant Publications; Willard Jabusch; Jan-

Lee Music; Shalom publications; Songs & Creations; and Vernacular Hymn Publications. "I was told that it would never work," said Fitzpatrick. "Publishers would not work together. But it did work until lawsuits against the Church dominated." The CSC model was later successfully employed by CCLI (Christian Copyright Licensing International [Protestant]) and New Dawn licensing (Oregon Catholic Press).

Catholic liturgical music continued to evolve in the 1980s. NALR was now a major Catholic music publisher and their growing roster of stars was impressive: Michael Joncas (b. 1951), Joe Zsigray (b. 1953), Grayson Warren Brown (b. 1948), Tom Conry (b. 1951), Paul Quinlan (b. 1939), Tom Kendzia (b. 1954), Cyprian Consiglio (b. 1958), and the group that continues to influence liturgical music today, the St. Louis Jesuits, who created a new standard of excellence with compelling and memorable Scripture-based songs. The Dameans, with new member Gary Daigle (b. 1957), went on to produce a critically acclaimed collection of ritual music, *Remember Your Love*. NALR was also home to two phenomenally successful products: the *Hi, God* catechetical series for children by Carey Landry and Carol Jean Kinghorn, and the *Glory & Praise* contemporary hymnal that became in the 1980s what FEL's *Hymnal for Young Christians* was in the 1960s.

GIA Publications enjoyed success with two outstanding new composers, David Haas (b. 1957) and Marty Haugen (b. 1950), and the company introduced two influential hardcover hymnals, *Worship* and *Gather*. GIA also published the internationally beloved music of the ecumenical Taizé movement, composed by Jacques Berthier (1923–1994).

World Library Publications was still trying to rebuild itself as a division of J.S. Paluch. WLP's founder, Omer Westendorf, with Robert Kreutz (1922–1996), composed a new hymn, "Gift of Finest Wheat," which was chosen as the theme song for the 1977 International Eucharistic Congress in Philadelphia.

In the 1980s, *Today's Missal* of Oregon Catholic Press became one of the most popular periodical missals in America because of its *Music Issue* supplement, which successfully obtained permission to feature the songs of a variety of composers, including the St. Louis Jesuits. Now known as OCP, the company would go on to build a roster of liturgical artists who would specialize in producing music for the diverse needs of the multicultural American church: Bob Hurd, Jaime Cortez (b. 1963), Christopher Walker (b. 1947), Bernadette Farrell (b. 1957), the St. Thomas More Group, and other composers too numerous to mention here. In the 1990s, OCP became an even bigger player when it acquired NALR's composers and copyrights.

Someday, all these publishers and composers will have their stories told.

FEL Publications struggled on, maintaining its licensing program even as its market share dwindled drastically. Finally, in 1984, FEL won a copyright infringement award of $190,400 from the Archdiocese of Chicago for making 1.5 million illegal copies, at the time the largest such award ever made in the United States. FEL also won an attorney's fee award of $135,697, which was the largest attorney fee award in a copyright case up to that time.

The jury also awarded FEL $2 million for business interference by the Archdiocese of Chicago and $1 million in punitive damages. This $3 million award total was eventually reversed by a three-panel appeal board consisting of two Catholic judges. All money awarded to FEL went to its attorneys. Fitzpatrick then moved the company to Las Vegas.

With the loss of the final appeal in 1990, Fitzpatrick decided to sell what was left of the FEL song catalog to the Lorenz Corporation, a major Protestant music publisher based in Dayton, Ohio. Without the songs of their best-selling artists (the Dameans, Ray Repp, and John Fischer,[19]) the FEL catalog was a pale shadow of its former glory. However, it still had "They'll Know We Are Christians" and that was the song that Lorenz wanted above all.

Fitzpatrick knew it was time to move on. The industry he helped establish had now grown beyond both his English chant and the 1960s Folk Mass sound. After delving into real estate as a sales agent and then broker, Fitzpatrick found a new career as a chemical dependency and domestic violence counselor licensed by the state of Nevada, where he teaches men and women who are arrested for domestic violence abuse. Instead of jail, the offenders elect to attend six months of weekly classes at various counseling agencies. Fitzpatrick supervises several of these agencies and teaches the class on living skills and relationships.

The slow demise of the Folk Mass movement's pioneer publishing company seems sad, but Thomas Cook, longtime FEL staffer, puts the litigation years in perspective.

> Ultimately, FEL suffered from the drawn-out litigation. It was one of the major factors for FEL going out of business. But the lawsuits did a great service for the other publishing companies and for the Church. It woke up the conscience of the Church. There are very few people today who would publish or reprint anything without making sure they had copyright clearance. Frankly, I think publishing companies today owe a debt of gratitude to Dennis for having the courage to challenge copyright piracy when others did not. I can't recall which companies in particular, but he did speak with other publishers, asking them to join him, and nobody was willing to take the chance and the risk. We eventually lost, but in the process we raised the conscience of the people and changed the situation. The other publishing companies are enjoying the benefits now.[20]

What began as a spontaneous and optimistic worship experience sung in the joyful and empowering folk music style of the 1960s was transformed into the big business of number crunching, contract points, marketing strategies, and sales projections. The fledgling Folk Mass movement grew up and became the Catholic music industry, with all the attendant loss of innocence and naïveté. There was no going back.

1 "Hope It's Not Too Late" by Ray Repp, © 1969, Otter Creek Music. Published by OCP. All rights reserved. From his LP album, *The Time Has Not Come True*.
2 Leonard, Timothy, *Geno: A Biography of Eugene Walsh, S.S.* (Washington, D.C.: Pastoral Press, 1988) 83–84.
3 "Missalette" is a relatively new concept that J.S. Paluch attempted to copyright. A Catholic worship aid modeled after the personal missals of the pre-Vatican II era, missalettes are published in periodical form, to be replaced after a fixed time. Originally called *Monthly Missalette,* the Paluch worship aid is now published by liturgical season and features the priest's prayers, the Scripture readings, the Order of the Mass, and a selection of hymns in a convenient layout that enables the person in the pew to follow the liturgy easily. Several other publishers have produced similar works.
4 For a fuller account of the birth of the Contemporary Christian Music industry, see Charlie Peacock, *At the Crossroads* (Nashville, TN: Broadman & Holman Publishers, 1999) 41–66. See also www.maranathamusic.com.
5 To find the 2009 equivalent amount for the sums quoted in this chapter, multiply dollar amounts by 5.
6 Hawkes' letter, dated February 23, 1976, said in part: "We have been advised by our attorneys that we should inform all pastors in the Archdiocese [of the copyright laws] so that they will understand the risk of assembling songbooks from copyrighted sources without having the approval of the copyright owner. It is suggested that each pastor consider independently what he may wish to do under the circumstances…. We should have in mind that in justice the composers of these songs that we are using are entitled to be compensated for our use of their songs. That form of compensation is usually in the royalties they receive from the sale of their songbooks so that when we use these songs without their receiving some compensation they are not being treated justly. Consequently, we should not look upon the claim as made by the owner of the copyright as being improper or in any way unconscionable."
7 Knoedelseder, Jr., William K., "Church Music: Case of the Sunday Suit," *Los Angeles Times*, Sunday, November 27, 1977.
8 Ibid.
9 An FEL brochure featuring a Fitzpatrick article, "Why Lawsuits with Churches?", was mailed on August 1, 1975 to all Catholic parishes and schools in the United States and Canada. Fitzpatrick wrote: "We are convinced that an unwholeness in our spiritual condition exists that permits worship stealing to take place. We have exhausted all remedies, short of exposing this condition to the light of truth in a court of law."
10 Knoedelseder, ibid.
11 Greeley, Andrew, from his Universal Press Syndicate column, October 1976.
12 The NCCB/USCC (now known as the United States Conference of Catholic Bishops [USCCB]) is an association of bishops representing all the Catholic dioceses in the United States. The Conference constitutes the authority of the Roman Catholic Church in the US "to unify, coordinate, encourage, promote and carry on Catholic activities in the United States; to organize and conduct religious, charitable and social welfare work at home and abroad; to aid in education; to care for immigrants; and generally to enter into and promote by education, publication and direction the objects of its being." From the USCCB website: www.usccb.org.
13 The named archdioceses and dioceses were Arlington (VA), Boston, Brooklyn, Buffalo, Chicago, Cincinnati, Cleveland, Denver, Detroit, Fort Wayne-South Bend (IN), Green Bay (WI), New York, Phoenix, St. Augustine (FL), and San Francisco.
14 Fitzpatrick interview, ibid.
15 Knoedelseder, ibid.
16 Winiarski, Mark, "Royalties Battle: Dameans Suit Claims FEL 'Deprives Artists.'" *National Catholic Reporter*, February 16, 1979, Vol. 15, No. 17.
17 All figures and court arguments in this chapter from Winiarski, ibid.
18 Fitzpatrick interview, ibid.
19 Fitzpatrick had earlier sold the songs of John Fischer to publisher/songwriter Johann Anderson, who featured them in the popular Christian music songbook, *Songs of Creation*.
20 Interview with the author, Los Angeles, California, December 28, 2003.

Epilogue
"Is There Any Word?"

We celebrate promises made by the Lord
to stay with his people in time,
But time hardens memories of promises made
between hearts that drank of one wine.
So now we are waiting again for the Lord,
and our fleeting hearts beg for some sign.

Is there any word from the Lord?
All our hearts have spoken must be heard.
And we long for some reply from the Lord who bore our lives,
and our waiting hearts still sigh for some word.[1]

—The Dameans

On October 13, 1988, I was in a yellow school bus with a group of pastoral musicians and liturgists that included composers Mary Frances Reza and Father John Schiavone (b. 1947). It was the annual meeting of the Federation of Diocesan Liturgical Commissions (FDLC), and we were wrapping up a marvelous evening of liturgy and dinner at Mission Basilica San Diego. Now we were on our way back to our hotel.

Sitting next to me was my old college buddy, Bob Hurd. I had not seen Bob since 1978, but now, by sheer coincidence or grace (I choose the latter), we were back together, working as pastoral musicians at Saint Leander's Church in the Diocese of Oakland, California. In the intervening years, Bob had distinguished himself as a successful liturgical composer and he invited me to join him at this FDLC conference to support him musically as he presented a workshop on his new bilingual Spanish and English music for the multicultural Church. We were three years away from composing *Mass of Glory*.

To pass the time on this pleasant bus trip, a friend across from us started singing chords — or at least bass lines. He sang the ubiquitous "C – A minor – F – G7" chord pattern and everyone in the bus chimed in by singing that old childhood piano favorite, "Heart and soul, I fell in love with you. Heart and soul, the way a fool would do…."

Suddenly, our friend the chord intoner started singing, "Here we are, all together as we sing our song…."

That did it! Amidst howls of laughter the whole group launched into raucous renditions of old Folk Mass favorites: "Here We Are" segued into "Sons of God" — of course! "Shout from the Highest Mountain" was sung as "JUMP from the highest mountain…." Our version of "They'll Know We Are Christians" included that unforgettable grade-school parody verse: "We will fight with each other, we will fight tooth and nail…." And then there was that immortal sending forth song: "The Mass is ended, go to the hall. Coffee and donuts are served for all…."

By the time we arrived at our hotel many of us were in tears from laughing so hard. We also felt a common bond that had scarcely been expressed since the end of the 1960s. The Folk Mass was a part of our youth and inspired our decision to become pastoral musicians. We cut our teeth on these songs and, although much of this music now seems trite, there is no denying our fondness for the Folk Mass and its place in our Catholic musical formation.

At some point, the folk-style music that was originally permitted only for youth became the mainstream style for the general parish community. Some parishes still refer to their contemporary choir as a "folk group," but that is a misnomer since folk music is no longer the dominant style in popular or liturgical music. Indeed, Lucien Deiss' 1970 prediction — that "the encounter between the music of 'today's world' and the music of tradition should result in a new creation" — proved to be on the mark. Today's mainstream liturgical music as performed in the parishes is a hybrid of the folk, soft rock, and traditional hymn styles, with a growing incorporation of the diversity that makes up the American Catholic Church, as expressed in the music of the Hispanic, Vietnamese, Filipino, African American, and other communities.

What is the legacy of the Folk Mass? It depends on whom you ask. We're still a little too close to the phenomenon to give it proper historical perspective, but after forty years some opinions have emerged.

In 1967, many Catholics were already lamenting how the loss of the Latin liturgy dismantled a perceived sense of pre-Vatican II unity. First, before the Council, many believed that one could go to Mass anywhere in the world and still feel at home because of the Latin. This was a misunderstanding because Eastern Catholics have always celebrated Mass in their own vernacular: Greek, Coptic, Armenian, and more. Secondly, the changes led to a fragmentation in parish liturgies based on preference for style (Folk Mass, traditional choir Mass, silent non-music Mass, etc.). Father Clarence Rivers, at the height of his career, made the following observation:

> The logical question is whether lovers of the popular, the classical, the folk, the jazz can endure one another's tastes, can love and associate with one another. If the command to love can require that I be willing to be present to my neighbor of different color or nationality, can it not also require that I be willing to be present to my neighbor of a different cultural background?
>
> If an integrated cultural situation is not immediately comfortable, or even if it is a painful process, we ought to remember that love will always require some sacrifice.[2]

By 1973, the atmosphere of change had settled down somewhat with the promulgation of the *Missal of Pope Paul VI*. Liturgist George Devine wrote:

> At this writing, we seem cut adrift from Rome and Peoria alike, in a way. While we have surely not preserved the pre-Conciliar forms of musical worship on any grand scale, we are not so boxed into the Folk Mass rage as we were in the late 1960s. Most of the good features of the Folk Mass experience, thank God, seem to be surviving. Most of the aspects of it that were merely superficial and transitory, or just downright awful, are on the wane (equal gratitude to the deity for this). As recently as five years ago, were a group of my college students to experience (i.e., hear and/or sing) a Joe Wise or Sebastian Temple folk-hymn, most of them would be enchanted by it and a few would even have tears of emotion running down their cheeks; today, most of them yawn and a few even wince. We are making progress.[3]

In 1990, Thomas Day (b. 1943) began questioning the legacy of the Folk Mass in his book, *Why Catholics Can't Sing*, a work that continues to stir debate. He commented on the modern liturgical songs that followed in the wake of the Folk Mass.

> The victory of the folk style, reformed or otherwise, is so great and so blinding that many people cannot see beyond that apparent success to what could mildly be called the *problem* of this music: simply put, nearly all of it — no matter how sincere, no matter how many scriptural texts it contains — oozes with an indecent narcissism. This folk style, as it has developed since the 1960s, is Ego Renewal put to music....

> Christianity was founded on the principle that God is indeed our friend, but those casual, la-dee-da melodies, the easy familiarity of the music, and the let-me-show-you-how-sincere-I-am expressiveness all indicate that God is our *little* friend and very much under our control, on the end of a leash. As one music critic put it, the music seems to say (to our little friend), "Have a nice day, God."[4]

In 2004, the music of Ray Repp was re-released on CD by OCP. The composer, still dedicated to the Council's call for social justice, commented on the Folk Mass legacy and his role in it.

> They say that because of people like me, we lost the dignity of our wonderful ritual. I feel like I only tried to do something meaningful. In the beginning it was an accidental kind of a thing. And then later, when I got into it "professionally," I intentionally tried to take the position that as we gather around the table that we call the Eucharist, we are called together to somehow focus on the mission of the Gospel, which is basically to go and love one another, and to do something to make this place a more responsible world, a more just world.

> Okay, I can't write polyphony. I'm not Palestrina or Mozart, or even some of the more contemporary, wonderful composers. And I'm in no way trying to convince people to always use folk music.
>
> So many liturgical musicians look down on the folk thing and say, "That's just not good music." I'm not going to argue with them! But what about dealing with the theology in their more "sophisticated" music? Too often they're just re-hashing some poorly translated psalms or alleluias to death, and I'm thinking, "Where are we? Let's put it all together in some kind of honest way."[5]

Now, as in the 1960s, the Folk Mass continues to polarize liturgists, pastoral musicians, and Catholics in general. I believe the Folk Mass was and still is a convenient lightning rod for supporters and detractors to comment on the reforms of the Second Vatican Council. That is the *real* issue. Outside of the vernacular, the Folk Mass (and its progeny, contemporary liturgical music) may very well be the most visible and enduring effect of *aggiornamento*. As such, it is an easy target that deflects criticism of the Council itself.

The late Monsignor Fred McManus (1923–2005)[6] wrote poignantly about this in his final article.

> Today there exists, in high and low places within the Catholic community, a body of "restorationists" and "traditionalists." It is a body that I suspect remains a small minority, however misguided and certainly noisy.
>
> The complaints may be easily dismissed as attacks on the Second Vatican Council and its two bishop presidents — John XXIII and Paul VI — and, indeed, on Pius XII, who had already agreed to principles of liturgical reform before the Council was even imagined.
>
> Today I mention this attack — this dissent, as it were — only to make a further point: We should recognize, once for all, that the Church has moved forward liturgically in ways from which it cannot retreat. These include the noble simplicity restored to the core Roman liturgy (varied, flexible, and eclectic as it remains), celebrations in the (preferable) vernaculars, a vastly richer and improved proclamation of the Scriptures, familiar and welcome ritual changes, at least a firm principle and starting point of inculturation, and, above all, participatory involvement of everyone in the Christian community at prayer, and on, and on....
>
> Doubtless the story in John Cornwell's *Breaking Faith* is true: There is a parish where the height of the Christmas liturgy is the singing, at the words of institution, of "Happy birthday to you...happy birthday, dear Jesus...." (John Cornwell, *Breaking Faith: Can the Catholic Church Save Itself?* (New York: Penguin Books, 2002). Doubtless, too, this kind of banal, bizarre, "schmaltzy populism" can be matched in many other

> places. Yet I am going to draw just the opposite conclusion from the expected one and propose that the liturgical renewal of song and music has demonstrated tremendous development and progress. Every alleged weakness or aberration can easily be matched by manifold positive signs in the living communities of Christian workers....
>
> We should mention, as a positive sign of progress, the deep contrast with our recent past, especially in ordinary American parishes. Sociological studies or anecdotal recollections would help, but the truth is simple enough: Aside from cathedrals and very exceptional parishes, aside from some monasteries and seminaries, the liturgical music fifty years ago was far inferior to what we possess today.
>
> Commonly in those days, there was a single sung Sunday Eucharist of modest quality in a parish (with, by the way, very few communicants) along with a "children's Mass" with hymns of modest quality. Even in the exceptional community, the occasional use of classical polyphony was chosen almost to distort the structure of the mysteries — with an elaborate and lengthy *Sanctus,* for example, and a *Benedictus* after the words of institution. This might sometimes have been music of high quality, but it was more suited to a religious concert and was often a disproportionate distraction from the Eucharistic action....
>
> Far from turning back, far from hesitating or standing still, we move forward and upward. We see liturgical music as the movement of the Holy Spirit of God in the Church.[7]

In these pages I have tried to place the Folk Mass within the historical context of the liturgical reform movement, the social and political forces of the 1960s, the secular folk music of the day, and the way American Catholics reacted to the Second Vatican Council. The Folk Mass composers, much like their secular folk music counterparts, were only giving voice to the excitement and exhilaration of the times, as an ancient Church suddenly opened its windows to the changing winds of the modern era. It is my firm belief that the Folk Mass can only be fairly criticized when studied within this context.

Yes, mistakes were made. Hundreds of years of a beautiful liturgical music tradition was, for the most part, thrown out like the proverbial baby in its bathwater, all in the name of progress, whether well-intentioned or not. New music was often created on the fly, with little or no thought given to the liturgical principles that guide composing today. Publishing companies were run by church musicians dealing with the challenge of creating a new industry from scratch. On the plus side, they certainly had a good sense for the kind of music the people wanted to sing.

The people have spoken. As mentioned in chapter 11, only a handful of Folk Mass-era songs are still sung at liturgy today. That alone says something about how contemporary liturgical music "grew up" from its formative years. But on the morning that I wrote these closing remarks, I was at my parish, Holy Trinity Church in Beaverton, Oregon, helping to lead my youth choir at our 11:15 Sunday liturgy. This is a group of whom I have been most proud, teen singers and musicians who take seriously their call to lead our assembly in song. Keep in mind that this youth choir does not sing at an exclusive Sunday evening "Youth Mass." The 11:15 is a regular parish liturgy for all age groups: families with small children, teenagers, young adults, and senior citizens.

For the preparation of the gifts we sang Sebastian Temple's "Make Me a Channel of Your Peace." Although rarely sung at our parish, it happened to fit the readings of the day and was selected by our planning committee. Our ensemble's sound is definitely not traditional "folk." We have piano, bass, drums and electric guitar, with occasional woodwind and strings, plus the energetic spirit of our teen singers. As we launched into the song I was immediately struck by the volume and quality of our assembly singing. I looked up from my piano into the congregation and noticed something I don't see too often in a Catholic church: *everyone* was singing!

I saw a six-year-old girl leaning close to her mom as they shared the parish hymnal, both of them singing together. I saw several teenage girls singing enthusiastically, next to a cluster of senior citizens who sang the words from memory. Even that quiet gentleman who keeps to himself and sits in the same pew every Sunday with his arms folded was singing along. Our priest sang with the people as he received the gifts of bread and wine. It was quite stunning to behold the full, conscious, and active participation of my parishioners, singing this beloved Folk Mass classic.

And then I thought about Sebastian Temple, of his enthusiasm for music ministry, his poverty and personal struggles, and how his song touched the world through Princess Diana. Suddenly, it all made sense. *This* is the legacy of the Folk Mass: a Church united across all generations, gathered together to celebrate the Eucharist, in their language, in their song. Naysayers may criticize it all they want for the way it married the sacred with the secular, but the Folk Mass empowered the Catholic people to sing, not as an audience but as a community who is one in Spirit, one in the Lord.

The fire still burns.

---

1 "Is There Any Word" by Darryl Ducote, ©1971 by Damean Music.
2 Rivers, Clarence J., *A Mass for the Brotherhood of Man,* liner notes from the LP jacket, 1967.
3 Devine, George, *Liturgical Renewal: An Agonizing Reappraisal* (Staten Island, NY: Alba House, 1973) 116.
4 Day, Thomas, *Why Catholics Can't Sing* (New York: Crossroad, 1990) 60, 64. One might take note that Day's pointed observation could be equally applied to the Protestant-oriented Contemporary Christian Music.
5 Interview with the author, October 1, 2004, Portland, Oregon, by phone to Ferrisburg, Vermont.
6 Monsignor McManus has been quoted throughout this book in his capacity as the founding executive secretary of the Music Advisory Board for the Bishops Committee on the Liturgy.
7 McManus, Frederick R., "Far from Turning Back," *Pastoral Music*, Volume 29:1, October-November 2004 (NPM).